Even though people are leaving church systems i deep, meaningful, and simple life of faith. Matt K he does what he does best—tells honest stories nected and less alone in our wrestling and in our trusted and seasoned guide on the path "home" s clearly in *Bring it Home*: "maybe we can find God by finding ourselves."

Kathy Escobar, co-founder of The Refuge and author of *Faith Shift: Finding Your Way Forward When Everything You Believe Is Coming Apart* and *Practicing: Changing Yourself to Change the World*

Matt Kendziera's tender book is a balm to those who long to come fully alive. In beautifully crafted short chapters, he vividly describes the journey involved in accepting the mystery of the divine in ourselves and finding our own unique, "beautiful, flowing river of faith." His tales are filled with energy, humor, and humility. I laughed and cried and couldn't put it down!

Anne Evans, leadership group member at Ashoka

What a life provoking surprise this turned out to be! I laughed out loud, had moments of reflective tears, but all throughout I was slowly being drawn into the invitation of becoming— more accepting of my own journey, more deeply of others, and more open to the acceptance of God's acceptance of us all. This is not a "church bashing" piece. This work slowly turns into a mirror and whispers, "LIVE!"

Scott Jenkins, creative director of The Celtic Way, chaplain, and pastor emeritus

Bring It Home—here's a spiritual memoir that will make you laugh as it touches your heart. Matt Kendziera knows where to find you, and how to help you find what you're looking for.

Brian D. McLaren, author of *Do I Stay Christian?*

Everyone has, at least once, felt the bottom fall out of our worlds, our compasses spinning, with only despair for company. When that happens to someone you love, you'll want them to have a guide as humane, honest, funny, heartbreaking, and heart-enlarging at Matt Kendziera. In his company, all of us can find direction, and a path to bring our full selves home.

Raj Patel, author, academic, and filmmaker of *The Ants and the Grasshopper*

The familiar and stable settlements of church, belief, and security are being transformed into unfamiliar and dynamic paths of doubt, deconstruction, and unknowing. Right now, we need guides who have experienced this path, can show us how it unfolds, and even reveal how there is more joy and peace ahead. This is who Matt is and what this book can be for so many people. The wisdom and authenticity within his story can call us further ahead and back home at the exact same time.

Kevin Sweeney author of *The Making of a Mystic* and *The Joy of Letting Go*

Bring It Home

Bring It Home

The Adventure of
Finding Yourself after Being
Lost in Religion

—————◆—————

Matt Kendziera

lakedrivebooks.com

Lake Drive Books
6757 Cascade Road SE, 162
Grand Rapids, MI 49546

info@lakedrivebooks.com
lakedrivebooks.com
@lakedrivebooks

Publishing books that help you heal, grow, and discover.

Paperback ISBN: 978-1-957687-04-9
eBook ISBN: 978-1-957687-09-4

Printed in the United States of America

This book is comprised of personal stories. It reflects the author's present recollections and information gathering of experiences over time. Some names and characteristics have been changed, some events have been compressed, and some dialogue has been recreated.

Library of Congress Control Number: 2022942593

Front cover: ©iStockphoto / michaelkemter.com
Book cover design: Jonathan Sainsbury // 5.5×8.5design

To my Suzie Kay,
the adventure continues!

Contents

Introduction

We shall not cease from exploration.
And the end of all our exploring.
Will be to arrive where we started.
And know the place for the first time.
—T. S. Elliot

IN THE LATE SEVENTIES AN event happened that would change the course of history for one small boy in a very large world. One day I was riding my Big Wheel around the block with my older brother in a small town just outside of Madison, Wisconsin, and the next day we were loading up in the back of a red station wagon, heading to a place that would from that point forward carry the title of home. Passing into this new town limits for the first time, I was enveloped in the arms of a community that taught me how to live, believe, doubt, and be. Though I had no idea at the time, that move of less than seventy miles shifted my entire world.

Boscobel finds its place in the world surrounded by rolling bluffs in southwestern Wisconsin, along the Wisconsin River just twenty short miles before it accepts its destiny as part of the great Mississippi. The river, unlike the town's population, is ever changing. One day you can walk safely from one riverbank to the other, and the next you find yourself being carried downstream, the water denying you any foothold. During my fifteen-year tenure in Boscobel, this river swallowed up the lives of several young people who made the grave mistake of believing she would be the same today as she was yesterday. I was spared, but I eventually saw a metaphor in it that helped me survive making a similar mistake in my spiritual life. We all get too comfy with what's familiar, one way or another, in life and faith. I've seen more than one person get swept away for not appreciating the shift in their reality, and I've been the guy desperately hoping my feet might find something firm enough to stand on again. There was a time in my life when I was confident I had the answers to so many of the big questions faith asks. I've had to admit my faulty thinking, and instead of giving up on God and faith altogether, I've decided to rethink the foundation on which I stood.

Boscobel has some rich history. It can be thanked for those Bibles in the top drawers of every hotel you have stayed in. Some travelers once met in the now historic and broken-down Boscobel Hotel, not knowing that their chance meeting would be the conception of a dynamic organization called The Gideons International. If you have ever been handed a pocket-sized Bible at a park, on a street corner, or on a college campus, you likely have met a Gideons distributor. As people pass by the sign indicating the Boscobel town entrance, boasting a population of 2,662, it is easy to miss the faded announcement proudly declaring the self-appointed and hotly disputed title of "Wild Turkey Capital of Wisconsin." (Incidentally, this was the claim that sent my grandfather into the woods with a gun for the final time, when what he thought was a turkey turned out to be another man. We are all thankful that the victim survived, but grandpa's freedom to carry rifles did not.)

When I speak to groups of people in my home state, I often ask how many have heard of this little town. There is always a smattering of hands that go up, and on the rare occasion a small "whoop" from a person who has some sort of connection. To most it is irrelevant and unknown. To some it is a place they drive through on their way to somewhere else. A select few call it home. But to me Boscobel is the capital of the world, my first love, and the architect and designer of who I have become. It is the place where I clumsily began to stack the building blocks of myself and my beliefs. Though many of those blocks have been changed out over the years, it is and always will be where I go back to whenever I need to rebuild. Whether in faith, relationships, or anything else, heading back to where it all started has always been my key. This book is not a story of a town, but of a boy who grew up wanting nothing more than to leave. This is exactly what I did the moment I graduated from high school, and ever since that moment I have been trying to find my way back.

———✳———

I do not recall a time in my life when spirituality and the idea of God wasn't important to me. This is something I can trace back to those early days growing up in small-town America. It's as if faith is built deep within my DNA. From as far back as my memory goes, I can find a desire for whatever it is that's out there beyond what we can see, think, or imagine. I also recall always knowing that somehow I could engage with the divine, that it was part of me and I was part of it. On some level, I believe, everyone is born with an understanding of and a connection to the divine; some eventually find language for it and some do not, based on our surroundings and influences.

As early as I can remember I had people in my life who were tasked with the impossible position of teaching me about God. Who is this God? How do we understand this God? How do we appropriately engage with this God? Since we were Catholics, my parents gladly passed on that responsibility to the experts, which in our case were the priest and my Catholic school teachers. Later in life this transferred to some older friends and then evangelical pastors, authors, and mentors. Everyone who attempted to teach me about God believed they were right. They believed that somehow they had an inner knowledge and understanding of this supreme being of the universe. They would speak with conviction and a desire for others to think the same way they did. It was as if the goal was uniformity— that there was a right and wrong way to believe.

As I began to look at religion throughout history, I found an unsettling theme. People of faith have always believed they were right about something that it is impossible to be right about. There can be no universal certainty in our understanding of God because the divine was never meant to be completely understood, only experienced. Sure, we can learn about faith and religion from pastors, priests, and authors, but at the end of the day we are all simply putting words to our experiences. And all our experiences are unique, which should, hypothetically, lead to a faith culture that reflects that.

If I have this deep desire for spirituality, yet I am surrounded by people who believe they are "right" about how that works (and history shows they likely are not), what am I left with? I am left with the place where it all began. I am left with myself. What if the only true place to discover God is within myself? What if the story of divinity is not rooted in ancient letters and writings but in the story of my life, and yours? Maybe the goal should not be a uniform belief system, but a faith that is uniquely our own. Maybe the goal is not for others to understand how or what we believe, but simply to see the results of our beliefs through living our lives. Not that we are the *only* expression of God, or that we should turn toward humanism or a "new age" ideal. But our belief should be rooted in the way we see the authors of the Bible and even Jesus himself living out their faith.

I grew up as a jazz drummer, and jazz music is something I love to this day. A jazz tune will start with the part that everyone knows, often called the *head*. After playing through the head a time or two, the musicians begin trading improvised solos over the chord progression of the tune. This can go on for quite some time, and eventually, whether the band leader calls it out or whether everyone just knows it ahead of time, there comes a point when the group has to *bring it home*. They have been artfully wandering around the form of the tune, and to get to the end they have to bring it back to the point it began. I have been artfully wandering around a theme of spirituality for quite some time now. And like in a lot of jazz music, there have been a fair number of moments when what is happening simply does not make a lot of sense. So instead of wandering endlessly, jumping from church to church, theology to theology, book to book, maybe it is time for us to *bring it home*. Time to find a place that actually makes sense. It's time to discover the divine right in the center of our own story.

For a while now I've sensed that the quest to discover God may best begin by rediscovering myself. I don't want to return to Boscobel as much as I desire to return to the foundation it built: a faith that was developed not through learning, but by living. To return to a God I found in the woods, not in a church. The pages that follow tell my version of a story that everyone has. It's a story of becoming who we were meant to be by tracing the clues laid out along the way. It's a story of discovering faith not through religion or church but through experiences, relationships, joy, sorrow, success, and failure.

We live in a world that attempts to tell us how to act, who to be, how to live, and what to believe. Social acceptability trumps dreams and desires most of the time. We care so much about how others view us that we carefully craft a false narrative so we will be accepted by those whom we desire to see us. When we are young, we are told we can do anything and become anyone. We are encouraged to dance, sing, and play. By the time we reach adulthood, we are told that being ourselves matters only if it fits the construct we are in. And if you follow along with what is expected of you, you will gain a lot but will almost certainly lose yourself. For me this showed itself primarily in the evangelical church, an institution that taught me I can be loved as long as I become less liberal, ask fewer questions, and accept only a select group of people. Unfortunately for me and for many around me, I chose this path for nearly two decades, knowing deep inside that I was losing more of myself every day. As I have spoken to people across the globe, I have discovered that I am not unique. Many of us have spent large portions of our lives trying to find acceptance by sacrificing our true beliefs. What if we all decided to try a new approach—one that is more authentic, honest, and messy? What if we took down the masks, grabbed the hand of the doubter next to us, and truly stepped forward in faith?

Digging myself out of the hole I allowed myself to be buried in is a process I am still in the middle of and may be for some time yet. But this book is an attempt to unearth the true and authentic parts of me. Much like my story, your true self and authentic beliefs may be buried pretty deep. What used to be so natural now may feel elusive or even absent. This book is a prayer that through my journey to find home you will find your own. I trust that you will at the very least be amused by the life I have lived and the people I have met along the way, but I beg you not to find yourself wishing it were your own. Instead, I hope it drives you to an invigorating exploration of your own story of life and faith. You were created for a very real and meaningful life and a deep connection to the divine. Digging up what has been buried can be the most thrilling adventure!

This book will not give you a blueprint to follow for having a fulfilling life. You will not find three steps to inner peace. You will simply find an ordinary story of a boy from somewhere you have probably never been, who has done things you likely have never experienced, with people you will almost certainly never meet. Yet as you journey with me, my desire is that you peel away the layers of who you are "supposed" to be to discover who you truly are. And that you can replace what you were told to believe with what you know to be true.

———✦✕✦———

The big red station wagon pulled up to a dark brown duplex on the edge of town. I opened the door, stepped out of the car, and looked around. In front of me was a winding and adventurous path that would include all the people, things, and experiences that tell the story of who I am, and who I am becoming, while helping me to discover the reality of the divine that resides in the place it never left.

1

Faith Roots

Growing up happens in a heartbeat. One day you're in diapers;
the next day you're gone.
But the memories of childhood stay with you for the long haul.
—*The Wonder Years*

A COMMON THING WE do with kids in our lives is ask them what they want to be when they grow up. It's not so much that we are asking them to create a career path by age five, but it's to discover what gets them excited. Kids are naturally drawn to fascinating things, which often makes their choices quite interesting. Many opt for construction workers, princesses, firefighters, or doctors. But none of those options were interesting to me, which is why adults who asked me that question got a nice little surprise.

If you are as shallow as I am, one of the determining factors in choosing whether to read a book is what the author looks like. I see a book that looks and sounds interesting, flip through the pages, and ultimately turn to the back cover to take a gander at the writer's picture. I have apparently decided what I want the person who speaks into my life to look like. If I am going to be fully transparent, that person usually has to look a bit like me, or at least a bit like someone I would want to hang out with. For example, if the author is wearing a suit and tie, the odds of me reading the book are minimal because, at the moment of writing this, I do not own a single suit. I must say I am extremely thankful for my less judgmental friends who have recommended books by people who do not look like me. I will always put recommendations above personal biases, which has led me to some incredible reads! I guess you could say I do indeed judge a book by its cover; the back cover, that is. If you peeked at the back cover of this book, which I bet you have (or at least I choose to believe you have so I don't feel like the only shallow one in the room), you can see that I am very tall and very thin. Some would use the word *scrawny* to describe me, but I choose *slim* as my desired adjective. My father is Polish and my mother is Czech, giving me very dark hair and a prominent nose. I'd suspect you decided to read this book because you know me, because you have a connection to my hometown, or because that picture somehow connected with you. The last one leaves me with a lot of questions about you.

———•:•———

One of the first trips I ever took with my family growing up was to a spectacle of a town called Wisconsin Dells. This is a place known worldwide for its plethora of water parks and random attractions. Huge water slides, strange gravity-defying buildings, vehicles that can drive on land and float through water, waterskiing stunt groups, and odd dome-shaped buildings are included in the eclectic variety of entertainment found in this young person's wonderland. As interesting as all these things were to me, there was one part about the town that grabbed my attention more than anything else. I walked into a gift shop and was immediately surrounded by Native American headdresses, moccasins, arrowheads, and jewelry. Seeing photos of warriors and chieftains made all the waterslides and attractions fade far into the distance. In this gift shop, surrounded by cheap T-shirts and inappropriate coffee mugs, I discovered what I was going to be when I grew up. I was going to be a Native American! For some reason no one felt it important to explain to me that heritage wasn't a choice and that I couldn't stop being Polish by wearing a loincloth.

So for years I was convinced that my future, or should I say my destiny, included teepees, horses, moccasins, and face paint. I even went so far as to cut up one of my dad's deer hides that was stored in our basement to create some Native American wearables. I would dress up and run through the forest surrounding our land looking for cowboys to battle and adventures to be had. When I would sit with my grandfather watching old Westerns, I always rooted for the Native Americans even though I knew they were destined to lose, both in the movie and in the reality of our current culture.

Although I am impressed that my parents were able to hold out as long as they did, they ultimately took up their position as dream killers by explaining to me that being a Native American was not a valid career choice. Away with the moccasins, away with the loincloth, and away with all my hopes and dreams for a bright future. I wiped the tears from my eyes, lifted my chin, and started to look for a different career option.

Around this time, I began to attend a Catholic grade school and was becoming fascinated with everything religious. I had attended the Catholic church since the day I was born, but going to school at a place attached to the church broadened my interest even more. The beautiful stained glass, the fascinating statues, the odd concept of drinking someone's blood and eating their flesh—who wouldn't find that appealing? All these things, along with the mystery of religion, were intriguing, but the greatest thing about the church and the school was the man at the top of the hierarchy. At Immaculate

Conception Church this man's name was Father Pat. He was living the dream!

First of all, he got free rein over all the cool stuff. He actually lived right next door in a building attached to the church called the rectory (which always sounded unfortunate to me) and could go into the church any time he pleased. Everyone called him Father even though he wasn't actually a dad and therefore didn't have to deal with any actual children. Everyone believed he knew all the deep inner realities about God, and no one ever questioned him. He got to wear all these spectacularly colorful robes, sprinkled people with holy water, smoked the place out with incense once in a while, and was the one guy who hypothetically could see the wine and water turn into blood. To top it off, a Catholic priest is not allowed to get married, which to the ears of a first grader sounded pretty damn great! If I couldn't be a Native American, then off to seminary for a life of masses, blessing people and animals, drinking wine, giving last rites to the dying, and being single!

One summer day my brother and I were outside playing when I came up with an extraordinary idea. I went into my dad's closet and grabbed his bath robe. I then headed to my room to grab my toy record player loaded with "Camptown Races." If you grew up in the seventies or eighties, you had this record player as well. The records were plastic with little notches that magically played music when the needle moved across them. Then off to the kitchen to grab a box of Nilla Wafers. I summoned my brother and told him we were going to mass. He hated church with the same passion with which I loved it but decided to go along with it because it was something to do. We headed outside (we were a progressive outdoor church), and I put on the robe, cued up "Camptown Races," and served Communion to my congregation, which consisted of, well, just my brother. Luckily, he enjoyed Nilla Wafers, so I was able to convince him to consume several pieces of Jesus' body in sugary wafer form. I traded in my loincloth to become a man of the cloth. This was it! I had found my calling. That is until we got a real record player and I listened to Michael Jackson and John Bon Jovi sing about girls in a way that made me feel a lot less interested in celibacy. So long crucifix, hello sex and rock and roll!

I am confident that I am not the only kid who had some interesting and strange ideas for the "What do you want to be when you grow up?" question. For years I brushed this part of my life off as simply a story that I could share with my kids one day and laugh about. A cute story about a kid who didn't know much about anything. But the more I shared the story, the more I began to connect with it. As I found myself thinking a lot about this early part of my life, I started to wonder why I was drawn to the things I was.

We are quick to dismiss kids' dreams and ideas as cute, believing that they will fade or go away when they realize they are Polish or attracted to girls. But the unique reality about this time in our lives is that we are not clouded by what others expect of us. No one is concerned about social acceptability, and no one is trying to encourage us to make a decision based on safety, security, or monetary gain. This is one of the only times in our lives when we are given the liberty to think and believe anything we want to, even if doesn't make sense in the context of the world we live in.

The truth is, I was and still am very much a "Native Priest." Once I realized that, I gave myself permission to explore the career path I first desired. Sure, I could never become a Native American, and the priesthood was not in the cards for me, but I connect very deeply with what those two figures stood for in my mind, in my heart, and in my soul. The Native American is the part of me that loves and

honors nature. My greatest joy and clarity come when I am surrounded by it. Being in a kayak on a river helps everything make
sense. The forest helps me feel connected. Riding my bicycle down
an old country road brings me joy I could never explain in words on
the pages of a book. My young perception of a Native American also
speaks to my constant craving for adventure.

I am an Enneagram seven, an "enthusiast," which means that for
me, the best idea is always the next idea. I have shared with my family that I have no plans of retiring, and I plan to skid to a stop with a
smile on my face when I die because I can't imagine a life that doesn't
involve the adventure of the next idea, project, or plan. The poet
Atticus once said, "I want to arrive at my funeral late, in love, and a
little drunk." That describes me well! People have said a lot of things
about me over the years, including but not limited to calling me the
Antichrist, but no one has ever been able to accuse me of settling for
ordinary or lacking bravery.

People who haven't seen me for a while often start by asking,
"What are you up to *now*?" instead of "How are things going?" My
parents call me an "entre*manure*" because "he does all sorts of shit."
For my birthday I rarely ask for any gifts but almost always give
myself the gift of enjoying nature by myself by taking a walk in the
woods or floating down a river. Adventure and nature make me feel
more alive and more myself than anything else. If I am in a shitty
mood, the answer is always the same—go outside or come up with a
new idea!

In the same way that the Native American represents adventure
and movement to me, the priest represents wonder and connection.
Father Pat represented a world filled with spirituality, where everything meant something. Everything he wore had meaning: the col-
ors, the symbols, every little statue and relic—all of it represented

something divine. The priest in the Catholic tradition is the one with a direct connection to God. As much as I loved the robes, the bells, and the incense, what I desired then and desire now is a direct connection to the divine mystery of the universe. My six-year-old brain put two and two together and was convinced that the best chance of this was through the priesthood.

I have met a lot of people in my life who like to put a date on the moment they began believing in God. This for many is called "salvation" or "conversion," two words that make me cringe because they represent so much that feels contradictory to what the divine represents. I want to honor everyone's journey, but this is something I struggle with because of the exclusive environment it inherently creates. Salvation becomes the card that members must hold to truly belong. Jesus seemed to care very little, if at all, about the "salvation" of the lepers, the poor, or the thief on the cross. He simply met their needs, encouraged them to keep quiet about what was happening, and let them know it was all going be okay.

My connection to God goes as far back as I can remember. It is something I felt in the walls of Immaculate Conception Church, but no more so than what I felt sitting on a hillside looking at the Wisconsin River valley. I have experienced this connection in crowds and by myself, in tears and in laughter, in pain and in healing, in Christianity and in paganism, in belief and in doubt, in love and in hatred.

The big things in life certainly hold meaning, but not more than the small things. The divine was profound in the moments when mine were the first human hands to touch and hold my daughters, and the divine is profound when I take the time to smell the crisp morning air. The divine is present and obvious in a passionate kiss and also in a slight touch. The universe has a way of opening itself up to us both in the midst of a meteor shower and with a gently falling snowflake. Life is not full of answers, but it is full of wonder and mystery! The divine is just as much in the mundane as in the majestic. The great mystery of the universe is seen just as clearly in the eyes of an inmate as in the work of a clergy member.

I never fell for the lie that Father Pat was somehow all-knowing or divine himself. The door from his home directly to the church gave him unlimited access to a lot of really shitty wine. Living alone with that sort of availability leads to obvious realities that I could never blame a human being for. His alcoholism showed him to be just as human as the rest of us. But I loved that he was willing to give up so much in order to experience the mystery of faith from a front-row seat.

Although the Native Priest has tried to hide many times, he is alive and well in me today. He refuses to bend his knee to authority yet willingly bows at the feet of mystery. He wakes up with a boyish excitement in his eyes, and as he combs his now thinning hair, he would much rather be smearing war paint on his face. He sees God in the eyes of his kids, senses the universe speaking to him while framing up a basement wall, and certainly senses divinity while enjoying a bourbon in a pottery cup while sitting on the front porch. And as he buttons up his shirt, he silently wonders what it must feel like to button the top button before sliding in a stiff white collar. As he puts on his buffalo plaid red wool coat, he feels the thick cloth of priestly robes fall over his shoulders.

As I ponder the Native Priest, I am reminded that we don't just get to experience the divine from afar; we also get to experience the divine from inside ourselves. In our most true and authentic spaces we will find it. In our most raw and vulnerable realities we will experience our life as a part of the greater whole. I find it fascinating that Jesus spent most his documented life in the streets, in the wilderness, and in the homes of those he interacted with. There was a time when one of his followers stopped him and turned his attention toward the buildings of the temple, the place where God was thought to be contained. Jesus didn't turn and walk back toward these "spiritual" places. He made a smartass comment and kept walking in the other direction (Matthew 24:1–15).

Over the past three decades I have been attempting to follow the footsteps of the Native Priest, but over and over again I've become distracted by the buildings and the organizations around me. I have been encouraged to follow the rules, pick and choose who is in and out, vote Republican, and believe that "pro-life" is somehow limited to the unborn. The reason Jesus walked away from all that bullshit is the same reason I have. It's because there is no wonder found there. It's because there is no adventure found there. And the only God in my mind who is worth following is one who runs through the forest and dips his toes in water at the river's edge. The God I desire to follow sits not on some fancy throne in heaven but on a wobbly chair at an old kitchen table. In what sort of alternate universe does it make any sense to honor Jesus by doing the things he never bothered to do?

A number of years ago the Native Priest walked out of a building with big crosses, video screens, fresh coffee, loud music, and polo shirts. He found where his loincloth had been stored (figuratively, of course, for the sake of all those around) and walked back into the wonder and adventure of the divine. This space is wide open with no boundaries. It's a space where I am no longer told what to believe, but where I get to believe what I experience. The good, the bad, the lovely, the heart-wrenching, and in all of it . . . the mystery.

Bring It Home

As we take this journey back home, an important place to start is the place we began. How will we ever expect to get home if we don't identify where home is? Sure, adults ask kids that "What do you want to be?" question to hear a cute or funny answer, but there is some truth behind whatever the answer is. Once we begin to grow up, factors such as societal pressures, money, and socioeconomics cloud our truest desires. When we are young, we consider none of these things, which means the answer that came out had a sense of authenticity.

Our journey back home needs to begin as far back as possible, when there were little to no obstacles. When you were asked that question, what were some of your earliest answers? As odd or crazy as it may seem now, is there any truth that can be found there?

Maybe you wanted to be a teacher because you are a person who loves to learn. Maybe you wanted to be a doctor because you have a desire to help others. Was it a farmer because you love the land, animals, or nature? It is possible that you wanted to be whatever it was because you admired someone who did these things, like a parent or a family member. That is not a bad thing. It shows that you had people to look up to in your life. But for this exercise, do your best to think of the things you desired that were unique to you.

Once you identify what you wanted to be when you grew up, ask yourself if you resonate in any way with that profession now. Not literally, but figuratively, like the Native Priest. My hope is that you will resonate with it deeply and in profound ways. But even if you can't think of what you wanted to be when you grew up, think about what kind of kid you were. Is that kid still alive in you now?

Odds are good that much of that wonder-filled child has been squeezed out of you over the years. We are told we can be anything, and then eventually we are informed that this was a cold-hearted lie, just like Santa and the Easter Bunny. To find our faith again, the first step is to discover who is trying to find it. If you attempt to find it as the shell of a human this world has made you to be what you will find is a shell of the faith you desire. It might look good at first glance, but just like a chocolate Easter Bunny, a bag of Skittles at the movie theater, or most hospital dramas on television, you will discover it to be hollow and lacking once you get into it.

I hate that in our culture, when people meet each other for the first time, one of the first questions we ask is, "What do you do for a living?" We are forced to then share our job positions, as if they're the same as our identities or even the things we resonate with. A better question would be, "What did you want to be when you were young?" or "What makes your heart come alive?" or "What is your biggest passion in life?" Step one in discovering the divine is to discover yourself. It's no wonder the church and evangelical Christianity failed me. It wasn't created for me. The Native Priest doesn't belong in a building being told by men in khakis how to think or what to believe. The Native Priest belongs in the wilderness. He finds God on the streets, in prisons, in schools, and in nature, not in a cozy chair, singing along with lyrics on a screen, with a nice cup of coffee in one hand and the other raised. He doesn't respond to four-on-the-floor drumbeats and thick synth pads; he worships through pipe organs, gritty folk music, and rhythmic drumming. We will find God in the same place we first found ourselves.

2

The Father, the Nun, and the Holy Smoker

Imperfection is beauty. Madness is genius. It is better to be
absolutely ridiculous than absolutely boring.

—attributed to Marilyn Monroe

MY EARLIEST SPIRITUAL INFLUENCES WERE three people whom I
affectionately call my holy trinity: three human beings who molded
my faith journey from as far back as I can remember and whose
effects I can see in my life to this day. I affectionately refer to them
as the Father, the Nun, and the Holy Smoker.

If you grew up living in a small midwestern town and had any
interest in God or religion, there were two choices. You could either
go to the Lutheran church or the Catholic church. A few extremists
called the Assembly of God church home, but most chose to ignore
their existence, dismissing them as the "holy rollers." The Jehovah's
Witnesses were active in streaks but likely lost heart as they discovered that most people could turn the lights out and hide for longer
than they were willing to stand outside and knock. The first and last
time they got my father to open the door was one of the few times in
my life I can recall unkind words flowing freely from his lips!

With roots deep within Polish and Czech heritage, my family was confident that Catholicism was not only the right way, but the only way! As I grew up, this led us to the only option: Immaculate Conception Church. The first point to be noted is that my faith journey began with both confusion and mystery as my young mind had no idea what either *immaculate* or *conception* meant. Since I grew up in a family that was not very open to difficult conversations, the latter of the two was something I would have to figure out on my own. Nothing like a church named after a knocked-up teenager!

Father Pat, whom you were introduced to in the previous chapter, was one of the most fascinating people I had ever met. If I had the option of spending one day with someone from my past, he would certainly be near one of my top choices. Father Pat was an Irish Catholic import who stood no more than five feet tall when standing up straight. He spoke with such a thick accent that only 60 to 70 percent of the mass was intelligible. Had the missalette (which, for my non-Catholic readers, is a small booklet that includes the order of the mass) not been available in the pews for reference, there would have been significant gaps in my knowledge base. Father Pat was famous for two reasons. The first is that during hunting season he was able to perform a Saturday evening mass in a mere twenty minutes to assure that the hunters could get in and out with plenty of time to prepare for the big day. Most of that preparation happened at a local bar called the Pour House, but nonetheless, the expedited mass was greatly appreciated. Some have argued that this is a tall tale because a mass generally lasts for close to an hour, but those skeptics may want to keep their voices down to avoid a bunch of drunk Catholic hunters at their doorsteps. Father Pat could have given any auctioneer a run for their money, and the congregational movement during Communion flowed with a sense of urgency not unlike the line to the men's bathroom during halftime at a Packers game. This seemingly small yet miraculous act endeared Father Pat in the hearts of the men of the church, which is a feat rare in the modern American church.

The other event that Father Pat became famous for was the annual Irish festival he brought to the Immaculate Conception School. One day each year in March all attention moved from the church down the block to the school gymnasium. The choir traded in their hymns for traditional Irish folk songs, school children prepared a host of Irish dances, the Blarney Stones (a Catholic, middle-aged version of a boy band) freshened up their harmonies, and the resident vocal teacher and opera singer dusted off "Danny Boy." The local lawyer, who was the only person from the University of Wisconsin system ever to major in music with the accordion as a primary instrument, rehearsed and led the band. Dancers and musicians from Ireland were flown in, and the school cooks transformed into Irish chefs, whipping up their best attempt at traditional corned beef and cabbage. Kegs of beer were brought in and dyed green while good and godly principles about gambling were dismissed as pull-tab game cards were peddled to fortune hunters. For one night each year the church turned into an absolute party! If you could ignore the middle-aged blonde woman who spent the evening dancing in the front row after a few too many colorful beverages and making loud, inappropriate comments to the performers, it was an absolutely lovely evening.

We cringed at the opera singer, laughed at the song about the beautiful young woman who turned out to be ninety years old, and clapped along with the resident yodeler. Although I did not make the audition to be an Irish dancer, one year one of the dancers got injured and I was the only option for a replacement. In my mind it went really well, but the reality is that after my cameo I was moved to the position of Irish band drummer and formally took the hint. It was likely for my own good, as I suffered an injury at the hands of a female dancer after one of the rehearsals. She didn't appreciate my gift of sarcasm regarding girls, the Irish, or dancing in general, and backhanded me in the face, causing an embarrassing and intense bloody nose! To add insult to injury, she just happened to be the daughter of some of my parents' closest friends. Drumming proved safer; there were never any women in the band.

As I reflect fondly on the annual Irish festival, my adult mind starts to wonder how much of the church budget was funded by beer and pull-tabs. If a church is struggling, maybe it's time to set aside our legalism and follow suit by setting up beer tents in our modern church parking lots! I'll never forget Father Pat—his beady eyes, red cheeks, crooked teeth, infectious laugh, and surprising temper easily provoked by grade school boys.

Maybe we should have seen this coming, but one day the dear Irish priest was ripped out of our community by the powers that be. Apparently, Father Pat followed the Irish Catholic stereotype by taking a lot of extra Communion—more blood than body, if you know what I mean. Extra Communion by the bottle eventually led to a problem, and all five feet of him was taken to a rehab facility never to be seen again.

After Father Pat was removed, the soul of our church left with him. We never recovered. The congregation tried valiantly to keep the Irish show going, but an Irish show without an Irish man proved lacking. Gone was the show, gone was the twenty-minute mass, all to be replaced by a priest who became famous for lulling us all to sleep each week.

The first few years my family spent in Boscobel were beautifully isolated. I stayed at home with my mom in our single-story brown duplex, and my days were filled with outdoor exploration, visits with the elderly neighbor lady, and dates with my dear friends Mr. Rogers and Captain Kangaroo. The B-in-the-mailbox routine never got old as the Captain put on his extensive beekeeping garb and headed out to the mailbox. Every time I'd beg him not to open that box, but my cries fell on deaf ears as he opened the door and looked in. Then he'd straighten back up and pull out a large capital letter B. The fun all skidded to a halt not long after our arrival when my mother decided she needed a job to help the family finances, which were largely going toward the house my dad was building for us in the country. That meant my brother and I would be heading to the Montessori preschool across the road from our church.

I'll never forget how hard I cried the day I was dropped off when my mom turned and walked out the door. The preschool was run by a tall, slender, dark-haired nun by the name of Sister Olive Jenab. Sister Olive is another person I would love to go back in time and spend an afternoon with. One thing that set her apart was her extremely creative menu planning. She worked with our resident British cook to come up with some very unique lunch menus. The most creative of her kitchen creations was the infamous "bean burger." What is a bean burger, you ask? Exactly what it sounds like. Disgusting.

My brother Jon, who was an extremely picky eater, found some incredibly creative ways to avoid the Montessori lunches. When salad was served, he simply shoved it in his pockets a little bit at a time until it was gone. I remember my mom's surprise one day when Jon forgot to empty his pockets before throwing his pants into the wash. She opened the washing machine only to find some very clean lettuce and carrots in the bottom of the wash drum. Jon's best method for food disappearance, however, involved the bean burger. There were twenty to thirty kids at the school, and for meals we sat on benches surrounding a huge rectangular table that filled the entire dining room. Kids were always jockeying for position, with legs and feet moving constantly under the table. Jon saw this not as a problem, but as an opportunity. He would pick his burger apart piece by piece and toss it onto the floor, into the sea of churning legs and feet. The burger pieces would disintegrate under the foot sea, and by the end of the meal the entire burger would be gone, with no evidence pointing back to the culprit.

A point that should be noted about Sister Olive is that in the few years that I spent there, I never saw her eat anything other than oatmeal. As we were busy choking down the surprise of the day, it was oatmeal for the dear Mother. Even as a young boy I felt a bit of resentment toward her for that. And today when I eat oatmeal, which I love, I always think of the tall, slender, striking nun in charge of watching over and feeding me for a few years.

Not only was Sister Olive a food hypocrite, but she was also the school disciplinarian. Although I wasn't the worst kid, I also was not the best. I can recall on more than one occasion getting my mouth washed out with soap for a variety of mishaps. If you have never had this opportunity in your own life, simply watch the portion of *The Christmas Story* where Ralphie drops the F-bomb while helping his father change a flat tire. His punishment looked identical to mine. The only difference is that my punishment was a public spectacle enjoyed by all the other children at the school. To this day I am unsure of what I could have possibly said since I am confident that I had yet to learn the rich language of rebellion that would usually warrant such a punishment. I also remember being forced to sit on the steps after getting in a tug-of-war with another boy that resulted in some broken glass and spilled blue-dyed water. I believe that memory has stuck with me simply because of the injustice that occurred when the other boy was acquitted of the crime, leaving me presumed guilty and all alone. It is not outside the realm of possibility that she had an issue with Polish kids.

Sister Olive was quirky, she was a hypocrite, and she was strict as hell. And because of these traits and so many others, I thought she was amazing. Flawed and fabulous! I did not have a crush on her like many young boys do with their teachers. She simply had control and command of every room she walked into. She was eccentric and unique, two qualities I value greatly to this day. Christian culture tends to value conformity, but Sister Olive Jenab helped me appreciate that individuality is worth preserving, for who we are matters more than who others want us to be.

The final part of my holy trinity was the leader of my Catholic grade school, Mrs. Haney. She taught the eldest students at Immaculate Conception. A chronic coffee drinker whose breath was simply awful and whose teeth were permanently brown, she was also a chain smoker. If she was outside, Mrs. Haney had a cigarette between her lips. This was quite beneficial to the other staff members as Principal Haney never asked for recess volunteers. She was always a more than willing observer, keeping the playground safe and her lungs filled with nicotine. Whenever I was called up to her desk or to her office in that smoked-out gravelly voice, there was only one thing on my mind: *Agree to everything she says so you can get away from her as quickly as possible.* Maybe it was a part of her master plan to lull children into agreement. Intentional or not, it certainly was effective.

This holy trinity was responsible for my early spiritual formation. For years I thought of them as cartoon characters in my story. But as I reflect on their influence now, I am struck by the importance of what they represent. They were all wonderfully flawed human beings. We live in a world in which religious leaders work hard to appear as if they have their shit together. They talk smart, dress well, drive nice cars, and raise perfect little Christian kids. They tell of a God who came for the weak but who expects the weak to get it together so they can be more accepted, more loved, and more valued. Their words speak of grace, but their organizations reveal duty and responsibility. So many have fallen under the weight of expectation. Don't swear, don't drink, don't have sex unless you're married. Give a bunch of money so a bigger building can be built and more staff can be hired and more people come and more power can be amassed.

My early experience of faith leadership was not with a person on a pedestal who pretended to be good and godly, but with three wonderfully flawed and broken human beings just like myself. Was Father Pat special and godly? Absolutely—and he was also a drunk. Was Sister Olive wonderful and purposed by God? Yes—and she was also a contradiction to everything she taught. Was Mrs. Haney a good administrator ordained by God? Maybe, but she was also a slave to three inches of rolled tobacco. These were people I could learn from and glean from without feeling as if what they had was somehow unattainable.

Jesus was a poor man benefiting from the welfare systems of his time and was homeless for a period. He was extremely ordinary and quite unconventional, especially that time when he sat down to weave together a whip while ominously staring at people selling goods at the temple before going Indiana-Jones crazy. We call him perfect, and I guess that is wrapped up in your definition of perfection. There is so much I don't understand about Jesus, and there is so much I question about his methodology, but I am most certainly drawn to all of him. The crazy quotes, the sleeping through a storm, the fishing stories. The man was not safe. He was also not all that put together, and he fit very few of the social norms of his time. If I am honest, I see more of the Father, the Nun, and the Holy Smoker in Jesus than I do the slick preacher in the fancy church with the loud music and moving backgrounds. I feel that if Jesus walked into that church, he would get a slightly menacing grin on his face before sitting in the chair against the back wall and slowly weaving another whip (probably while appreciating the fair-trade church coffee).

Bring It Home

On our journey home it is paramount that we look at the spiritual influences in our early lives. Many of us were driven away from church and faith by the very people who drew us toward it. Was that because of their failures, or because of our expectations? It was most likely a combination of both. Spiritual abuse tends to be a nasty combination of expectations, power, and confusion. We believe leaders have some sort of special ability to hear from God. Those leaders can internalize that expectation as the truth and believe themselves to have an authority that no human should have. The end result is a great deal of hurt, disappointment, sadness, and therapy.

If what drew you to faith was a person who gave you the impression that they had all their shit together, it is important that you let that go and see it for what it was: a misconception. If what drew you to faith was a group of people who were masters at manipulating your emotions, it is important that you let that go because it was far from true or authentic. If what drew you to faith was a person who guilted you into giving your heart to Jesus, please, by all means, take your heart back.

But if the person who influenced your faith was someone you admired because of their humility and love, who you were drawn toward in spite of their flaws that they never tried to hide, lean in! I lean in to the drunk priest, the hypocritical nun, and the chain-smoking principal because they are far more representative of myself and of God than some holier-than-thou man up front trying to act as if he is something he is not.

Take some time to sift through your spiritual influences. Lament and throw out those who need to be in the trash, and hold tightly to those who were true and lovely. And as you move forward toward your new quest of faith, commit yourself to no longer being influenced by people who don't make sense in the context of what it is you are searching for. There are plenty of slick talkers and good business-people in this world. We have no lack of politicians and egomaniacs. But do we really want these people to influence our connection to the divine?

3

Urine Trouble Now

A person without a sense of humor is like a wagon
without springs. It's jolted by every pebble on the road.

—Henry Ward Beecher

SECOND GRADE WAS A BIG year for me. It was the year I learned to
ride a bicycle without training wheels, the year when Joanna Zinck
used sign language to say "I love you" to me in the basement of
Immaculate Conception School before turning and running away,
and it was the year that a strange man at a friend's birthday party
lifted me up against a wall, pointed to a scar on his neck, and
informed me that being a smartass could cause me to get a matching
imprint on my own neck. All these things were significant and certainly deserve some contemplation, but one second grade event
stands out above all others.

For us young boys, everything was a competition. School work
was a competition, lunch was a competition, confessional time was a
competition, singing hymns was a competition, and farting noises
were most certainly a competition. You name it, we could compete
at it.

There was only one boy's bathroom at Immaculate Conception
School, and it was in the basement. I can tell what is going through

your mind right now! *He just got done saying everything was a competition, and now we are heading into the bathroom.* Exactly! The bathroom was typical of many old buildings. As you walked through the thick wooden doorway two light blue metal stalls were on the left. To the right were two wall-mounted white ceramic sinks. Instead of paper towels or blowers for hand drying, we had the community cloth towel that came out of a metal box on the wall. The cloth came out of the front clean and then looped around to the back, going into the box dirty. To this day, I cannot conceptualize any way that the dirty part of the towel does not soil the clean part. And to be perfectly honest, there really is no way to know what part of the exposed cloth is soiled. As far as I am concerned, we might as well have just had one shared community hand towel hanging from a hook. Safe to say we should all be grateful those contraptions are largely a thing of the past. Beyond the sinks were three urinals side by side. They were not the sleek new models that are small and hang off the wall; they were the traditional models that sink into the floor and offer a three-foot-high, foot-and-a-half-wide porcelain track to aim for. A nice-smelling blue urinal cake was tossed in the bottom, and a single white water tank was installed about six feet high on the wall directly above.

As a boy goes to the bathroom, he tends to look one of four directions during the process. Looking straight ahead is a modern trend brought about by smart bathroom advertising. At my school the only thing in front of a urinating little boy was a brick wall. Not much to look at. Option number two was to look down. This option is highly suggested for the sake of aim and overall functionality, and I highly recommend it for beginners, slow learners, and married men at home. The third option is to look to one side or the other, which, for the love of God, please don't accept as a valid option.

There is nothing worse than a stranger trying to strike up a conversation next to you at a urinal. And if you are that guy, please guard our humanity by getting some help, using the stall, or finding some friends! The final option is to look up at the ceiling or, in our case, at the white water tank. For one group of competitive little boys, looking up turned into a challenge too good to ignore. I don't really know how long it takes the average second grader to go to the bathroom, and I have no interest in researching the topic, but let's say thirty seconds for a safe estimate. A young mind can wander quite a ways in that amount of time!

One day I, along with my fellow second grade friend John and our first grade protégé Ben, were standing side by side at the urinals in the basement of Immaculate Conception Grade School when all our gazes simultaneously went upward. Chalk it up to God's humor or sheer coincidence, but that day our hearts melded with a common cause that only needed a brave soul to say it out loud for it to become a reality. On that amazing day the silence was broken when John, staring directly at the water tank, said in a tone that made it obvious he had been pondering this for some time, "Do you think I could pee on that white tank?" Oh to dream! Was this feat a real possibility or simply a pipe dream?

From that day on we began organizing coordinated bathroom breaks at the same time each day. We would meet at the urinals, myself on the left, John in the middle, and Ben on the right. Every day for several weeks we would unzip and stare up at the white tank. And every day the same question would be asked. "Do you think we could pee on the white tank?" A discussion would ensue about whether it was possible, using our limited urination experiences to glean from, most of which included some sort of outdoor urinating adventure. Today I stand over six feet tall, so the idea of being able to pee on something the same height as myself may not seem all that far-fetched, although I have my doubts about the plausibility of a forty-five-year-old being able to have enough pressure in his own tank to accomplish this. But when we were second graders, six feet up was a good two feet above our heads. Not only that, but in case you didn't know, boys don't pee from their heads—so add another couple of feet to the challenge and we are looking at needing a minimum of a four-foot lift to reach the white tank.

One day seemed like all the others. We met at the urinals at our agreed-upon time. We zipped down and looked up. One of us started with the question, "Do you think we could pee on the white tank up there?" And then it happened! An action that to this day still inspires me to go after my dreams! John, who, if you recall, had his spot in the middle, took one small step backward and leaned back. Oh my God in heaven, he was going for it. The stream headed up the glossy white porcelain and, just as it got to the top of the urinal, it died down at least two feet short of the goal. A roar of laughter came out of Ben and me, which was quickly met with a challenge: "I bet you can't do any better!" This challenge quieted our laughter and was gladly accepted. I took a small step back, leaned back, and had the same result. Ben found the same fate, even after seeing what failure looked like twice. This would not deter us. Tomorrow was another day.

We spent the afternoon drinking a lot of water and requesting an extra milk during snack break. As my grandfather would say, we had to go so bad that our eyeballs were floating! Our bathroom time had come, and there we stood in the same order as always. John was once again the first to make an attempt. Up he went, clearing the urinal without a problem but still ending a good foot short of the white tank. I was up next with a similar result, and Ben, who was a year younger, struggled to clear the top of the urinal altogether. This was our routine every day for several weeks. Drink water, meet in the bathroom, Matt, John, and Ben. Every day we would inch closer and closer to the tank as we honed our technique. The clear favorite was John, who had several inches on both Ben and me (inches up the wall for those whose minds just went in the wrong direction).

The incredible thing about this is that both Ben and I towered over John in height; he was the shortest kid in our entire class of eight people. Despite his clear disadvantage, he routinely bested us, making it farther up the wall every day. What he lacked in stature he made up for in water pressure. It's true when they say that size doesn't matter. At this point, there was no doubt in our minds that if we just kept going and got better at our craft we would, before the end of the second grade, touch the white tank with young and vibrant golden streams.

Every great story has a great villain, and this story is no exception. After having some success in our race toward the tank, we, like all athletes, began talking to others about our goals and aspirations. My best friend, also named Matt, was one of the people we shared this information with. The only problem was that Matt, like all of us, was a competitive little guy. Unfortunately for him, there were only three urinals, and they were all accounted for. As in many cases, success led to jealousy. Matt played along as if he were rooting for us or at the very least amused. But the reality was that he was the villain.

The very next day when John, Ben, and I headed down to the bathroom for our moment of glory, Matt headed straight to the principal's office to clue Mrs. Haney (the Holy Smoker) in on our little game. The three of us walked into the bathroom, took our rightful places, unzipped our pants, and leaned back with great hopes that today would be the day when the door swung violently open. A scowling Mrs. Haney came storming into the bathroom, teaching us all firsthand what it means to be caught quite literally with your pants down.

Because of all the commotion I can't recall exactly what happened from there, but it is hard to believe that we wouldn't have pissed all over ourselves trying to regain our composure. We zipped up, put ourselves together, and headed to the principal's office, where we were informed that there would be a phone call to our parents that evening. From that point on I had that sick feeling in my stomach that every kid gets when they know they are really in trouble. I spent the evening nervously waiting for the phone to ring, and to this day I am confident that Mrs. Haney intentionally took her sweet time calling just to make us suffer. It felt like an eternity. But finally, it happened. The ominous ring of the phone reverberated through the entire house, and, in slow motion, I saw my father pick it up. After a minute-long conversation, all the while looking in my direction, he slowly hung up the phone and told me to go to my bedroom. I burst into tears, ran into my room, and buried my head in the pillow.

As I anticipated what might come next—a spanking, getting grounded for the rest of the year, some good old-fashioned yelling—I heard something I most certainly did not expect. I heard laughter. First from my mother and then not long after from my father. It was not a giggle; it was full-blown, all-out belly laughing from both my parents. I can still remember my mother's flushed cheeks and watery eyes when she finally gained enough composure to come into my room. As she told me that Dad and I had to head to the school the next day to clean the bathrooms with the other boys, she couldn't squeak out the final word without letting out another giggle before turning and gently closing the door behind her. I laid back down and buried my head back in my pillow so they couldn't hear me laughing as well. The competition was over, but the memory will remain forever.

In our culture we have become really good at taking ourselves too seriously. When we are young we laugh and joke freely, but as we age our laughter suffers under the weight of responsibility. When was the last time you laughed so hard that your side hurt? Growing up, for me it was a regular occurrence. Marriage becomes serious, work is serious, finances are serious, parenting is serious, and faith is often the most serious thing of all. I mean, honestly, saving people from eternal torment in a fiery pit is serious business!

In all this seriousness, we lose all our joy. And joy is at the heart of true life. So often preachers point out the shortest verse in the Bible, which is "Jesus wept" (John 11:35). But we rarely hear about the reality that Jesus laughed, told jokes, poked fun at people, and enjoyed a good party. He loved a good party so much that he made sure the drunk people got drunker, which I would naturally assume brought about a fair amount of joy and laughter. I'm sure it also brought on some pretty significant hangovers, but let's stay focused on the good.

The only laughter I ever heard at church was when the pastor would kick off his sermon with a horrible joke he found on the internet. The congregation placated him with pleasant laughter to be kind before settling in for the part of the message where we hear the same crap over and over and leave feeling like shit because we are all sinners who deserve an angry God's wrath. Not much to laugh about there! But I did hear laughter at Immaculate Conception Church growing up. It happened two times each year. The first was during the annual Irish festival, where green beer was in abundance, and the second was during the annual pig roast, which included, of course, a beer tent. I have a feeling that if Jesus were hanging around Boscobel when I was growing up, he would have showed up at my church exactly two times each year!

Life is challenging. There are always plenty of hard things to focus on. But if we are unable to balance the hard with the hilarious, we will be crushed under the weight of it. When I turned forty, I looked around and started to notice how miserable many people my age seem to be. Most of them hated their jobs, which is a hard pill to swallow when you are only halfway through your working years. Their marriages had turned into roommate situations, save the yearly anniversary getaway which proved more disappointing each year. They lived for the weekend when they spent time on house projects or watching sports. Smiles and laughter seemed elusive.

So what is the answer? Maybe for you it's to have a drink once in a while—or maybe even more than once in a while. You could make happy hour a regular occurrence. For the non-drinkers a coffee happy hour is just as good. Laugh when you mess up and laugh when your kids mess up. Yes, of course, use everything as a learning opportunity, but you can do that and smile at the same time. Learning and smiling are not mutually exclusive. Tell stories and sit around campfires with friends. Leave projects until next weekend, or next year. Start believing in a God who laughs with you as opposed to a God with a constant scowl on his face. Stop going to things like lame church services that suck the life out of you. Quit your shitty job and start over. Take your spouse on a date. I could keep going, but I think you get the idea.

When my oldest daughter was a toddler, we would do this thing where, when she would misbehave, she'd have to sit on her bed for as many minutes as she was years old. My dear sweet Macia got lots and lots of time-outs as a young child. I would give her the proverbial talking-to, pick her up, and set her on the bed before going to the kitchen to set the timer. One time I did the first two steps but got distracted before getting to the kitchen. Less than a minute later I heard her cute little voice yell out from her bedroom, "Hey drummer boy, set the timer!" I immediately lost it and started laughing uncontrollably. The thing about laughter is that it is infectious, and she quickly joined in. I ran into her room, tackled her on the bed, and forgot all about whatever it was she did. Peeing on the wall, calling daddy a drummer boy: life hands you some real funny shit once in a while.

Bring It Home

I completely understand that when we are talking about spirituality that involves not only this life but all of eternity, it can feel a little daunting and overwhelming. But if we can't let down our hair a bit and laugh along the journey, we will become even more lost than we already feel. Life isn't supposed to be so serious, and neither is our spirituality.

Religious people can be the absolute worst at this. Historically, Christians have sought to suppress everything that brings enjoyment: sex, jazz music, rock music, dancing, swearing, drinking, and merriment in general. We are created to laugh. Why would we stop in the name of God?

I'll never forget when I was giving a message at a church service and I tripped over the word *success*, saying "sex" instead. My wife was in the front row, and she immediately pointed at me and said in full voice, "You just said sex in church." The whole place lost it. I'll also never forget when I was speaking at another church and I tripped over a microphone cord. Upon catching myself, I stood up and did my best version of a lyrical dance leap. People were laughing so hard it took a solid five minutes to get them to calm down. Yet another time I was emceeing a sold-out dinner theater variety show when halfway through the second act a gentleman placed a piece of paper next to me. I discreetly opened it and read, "Your zipper is down." I promptly looked at the audience, read it out loud, and zipped up in front of everyone. That was years ago, and every once in a while I will have someone stop me to tell me they were at the show where my zipper was down.

As you think back on things that have been difficult parts of your faith story, don't be afraid to laugh a little at how ridiculous some of those things were. One of the most healing moments happened to me while I was in front of a large audience telling the story of a bad church break I was in the center of. When I got to the part where I told them that the leadership team I hand-picked asked me to resign from the church community I started, the audience unexpectedly began laughing. They were able to see how ridiculous it was, which in turn helped me to see the same.

On your journey back home, surround yourself with people who make you laugh. And when the universe gives you the opportunity, take full advantage of it no matter where you are or what you are doing.

4

Showing Off

Knowledge is like underwear. It is useful to have
it but not necessary to show it off.

—Nicky Gumbel

GROWING UP IN SMALL-TOWN AMERICA in the late eighties and early
nineties came with all the stereotypical things you would assume.
Country music was king, which was proven by the fact that "Fishin' in
the Dark" was our class song. Feel free to look up the lyrics and you
will get a pretty good glimpse into the Boscobel High School class of
1994. Also, the prom court tuxes were complete with cowboy boots, a
cowboy hat, and a bolo. Guys liked their trucks, drank beer, and
chewed tobacco and to be honest the girls also liked their trucks,
drank beer, and chewed tobacco. Academics were secondary; several
of my classmates didn't make the necessary grades to walk across the
stage when it was all said and done. Sports were a big deal even though
most of the teams were terrible. During my senior year our boys' football, basketball, and baseball teams won a combined total of seven
games. I am sad to admit that I was on two of those teams. And I
probably don't have to clue you in on this one, but band and choir
were not the places where the cool kids hung out. The band room,
however, was most certainly the place I liked to hang out.

My saving grace is that I had a lot of success as a young musician, and the accolades were often touted by the local newspaper. (Props to *The Boscobel Dial.*) This, along with the fact that I was also an athlete, kept any unnecessary bullying at bay. One of the benefits to being a music nerd was that the male-female ratio was stacked in my favor; the band program had a four-to-one ratio, and the choir program, which I was guilted into joining since I was going to college to study music, had a total of two boys. Growing up in a small town with any amount of talent or determination allows you to quickly become a big fish in a small pond. And being a boy in the music program shrunk the pond and grew the fish even more. This was a reality I enjoyed a great deal, and I had no problem letting it get to my head.

In the band world autumn is the time you get to do most of your rehearsing outside thanks to football season. Football means marching band season, where we get to play epic pep-band classics like "25 or 6 to 4," "Eye of the Tiger," and "Iron Man" before taking to the field at halftime to perform our well-manicured three-song set list, complete with flag girls and choreography. I am confident we were at least better than the football team since they ended up accounting for zero of the aforementioned wins, but I am not sure we were all that much better based on our crooked lines and our melodically challenged brass section.

One beautiful afternoon the band was heading out to the field to rehearse for the upcoming halftime show. I grabbed my snare drum, put it over my shoulders, and headed out of the school building in front of the rest of the class. To get to the field we had to walk around a chain-link fence that stood maybe five feet tall. As I stood facing that fence with the entire band—mostly comprised of girls—behind me, something came over my teenage mind. You know how when you look back at your life and there are a handful of decisions you know will be discussed for years to come and maybe even show up in a book one day? This was one of those moments.

I decided it would be a great idea to jump over the fence. The logic of this alone was ridiculous. Even if I made it over—which, as a young man with springy legs, I was confident I could do—I wasn't going to attempt it with a snare drum attached to my shoulders. So I would have to jump back over the fence to get the drum and then walk around the fence to the field like everyone else. This logic did not factor into my decision-making process as I removed my drum and set it on the ground. Why would a young man want to jump over a fence? The first reason is that young men simply like to jump over things. I'll never forget one of my kids' grade school talent shows where a group of three boys showed off their talent of—you guessed it—jumping over things. Music played, and for several minutes they jumped over all sorts of random objects strategically placed around the gym. That day in high school there was a fence in front of me, so I thought I might as well jump over it. The second reason I did it is that somewhere in my not-yet-fully-developed brain I thought the girls behind me would think I was pretty awesome if I jumped over the fence. Ask any young woman what they look for in a man, and they will say good looks, a nice personality, a good sense of humor, and of course a strong ability to jump over random objects. What could possibly be sexier than that?

During autumn in Wisconsin you wear jeans. Jeans and a T-shirt, jeans and a sweatshirt, but jeans nonetheless. It is also important to note here that my parents never bought me any name-brand clothing. Not because they couldn't, but because they thought it was a ridiculous concept. And even though I agree with them for the most part, I now believe that you get what you pay for. I set down the drum and started a slow jog toward the fence. The narrative in my head regarding what the girls behind me were thinking was, *Wow, Matt is so hot and athletically gifted. He is so brave, attempting to leap over that chain-link fence.* The reality was more likely, *There goes Matt again. What a dumbass.* I approached the fence, picked up speed, planted my feet at the base, grabbed the top, and propelled my gangly six-foot adolescent frame upward. The approach was good; the takeoff was solid; everything was going as planned. I was flying over the top, winking and pointing at the girls (okay, that part is definitely not true) when suddenly I felt something catch. That something was the crotch of my cheap jeans on the top of the cold metal chain-link fence. And catch it did. It was as if that fence purposely grabbed my crotch and held on tight to teach this jackass a lesson. The next thing I remember is hanging upside-down from the crotch of my pants and staring through the fence at fifty to seventy band members, mostly girls, laughing their asses off and pointing. To make matters worse, as I tried desperately to release my crotch from the fence, the pants willingly assisted by ripping from said crotch all the way down to below my knee. There I was, laying on the ground, staring at the sky with my pants half ripped off, listening to the roars of my classmates.

My band director was laughing harder than anyone else and in an act of mercy allowed me to head back to the band room to locate some safety pins to take care of the disaster. I sulked back to the band room and did just that. I then had to go through the entire rehearsal and the remainder of the school day with pinned-up jeans trying desperately to keep my tighty-whities from being seen by the entire student body.

Bring It Home

As we make our way back home, it is tempting to want to show off our newfound beliefs. Most of us have felt misled or even taken advantage of, so expressing our new shiny thoughts and beliefs publicly feels like a way to stick it to those leaders who led us astray. When I started rethinking my faith outside of the confines of the evangelical church, I was happy to let anyone who would listen know my thoughts. Don't bother asking about hell; I'll just tell you. Want to hear what I think about inerrancy? No? Well, let me tell you anyway. I can assure you this was less than helpful and in most situations simply created some awkward tension among friends and family members. I wanted to let everyone know the errors of the Evangelicals. It's not that the questions and conversations aren't important. They certainly are. But if our motives are to be right or to tear down or to draw attention to ourselves and our new enlightened understanding, the conversations will likely prove irrelevant and even embarrassing.

Instead, let's turn our gaze to the hurting and the oppressed. Let's fix our eyes on the humans who have been traumatized by faulty religion and help them feel valued and loved. And as we speak out against the systems that caused this hurt and oppression, may we do it in a way that draws attention to the problems and not to the people or to our newfound rightness.

It's an unfortunate reality that if we are not careful, we can end up being a different version of what we hate. People will go from altar calls, literal Bible interpretations, and scapegoating gay people, Muslims, pro-choicers, and Democrats to throwing out the Bible and scapegoating straight white people, Christians, pro-lifers, and Republicans. Is one really any better than the other?

In the new field of faith deconstruction content, I have noticed that many of the most popular podcasts and Instagram accounts are the ones that are the most judgmental, negative, and crass. Drawing attention to correct thinking and freedom to swear and shit like that. So just to be clear, many seem to think that the road away from an exclusive, judgmental, closed-off system is to become exclusive, closed-off, and judgmental in a different way. I'm not convinced that is helpful. And as Mr. Rogers' mother told him, in difficult times, look for the helpers.

The path forward need not be filled with better, more correct theology, although that will be a piece of it. It does not need to be championed by new famous progressive Christians, although we are already starting to see them. Instead I am hopeful it will look a lot like Jesus by moving forward humbly, with strength and conviction. Calling out wrong with love and with a true desire for change. Trying to show off our beliefs and their rightness is what got us to this mess in the first place. And as you jump over the fence to a new way of thinking and believing, don't draw too much attention to yourself—because you just might snag your crotch on the way over and find yourself hanging upside-down on the other side. And that is embarrassing.

5
Finding Church

At first you might find that nothing happens there.
But if you have a sacred space and use it,
something eventually will happen.

—Joseph Campbell

I HAVE BEEN IN BEAUTIFUL cathedrals all over the world, climbed mountains, and stood before spectacular waterfalls, but there is one place that is more beautiful and majestic than all those combined. It is a small piece of property, less than an acre, outside a small town in northern Wisconsin called Phillips.

Immigrants, including my great-grandparents, were lured to this part of the state with promises of fertile land for farming. The land was cheap and the promise was too hard to pass up, so many came only to discover that these fertile fields were also filled with huge rocks. Drive around the farms on the outskirts of this small town to this day, and you will see field after field surrounded by piles of rocks that have been taken out of the soil to make it tillable.

Luckily I am a few generations removed from that backbreaking nightmare, and my experience with this little town is nothing short of sacred. My great-grandmother owned a small piece of property on the Elk River, and on this property sat what became affectionately known as "the old shack." The old shack was pretty much what it sounds like: an old house right on the river with no electricity, no running water, and of course no indoor plumbing.

The first experience I ever had at the old shack is one that I was too little to remember. When I was less than a year old, my family was staying there during what became known as the famous downburst of 1977. A downburst is when winds come down and across the land at the speed of a tornado but in a straight line. Hundreds of acres of trees were laid down by mother nature all in the same direction. My family quickly realized the gravity of the situation and all climbed down into the ten-by-ten-foot cellar in the old shack. My dad helped my mother down before handing my brother and me to her and hopping in himself. All of us, as well as the shack, were spared that day, which is good; otherwise this book would never have existed.

From that point forward that little piece of heaven was filled with stories and experiences that built on each other to make it a place of lore and legend. I can remember the excitement during the four-hour drive to Phillips. We would pull up to the shack and pass by the water pump, which was responsible for a scar that still can be seen above my eye from the time my mother didn't see me sneak up behind her while she was fetching some water. Just past the water pump was the screen door that marked the entrance to the tattered building. After we walked in, it would slam behind us with that sound that you hear in every great movie set in the country during the 1930s. The kitchen was nothing more than a sink basin since there was no running water. Past that was the wood stove, which was used both for cooking and heating, and the dining room. To the left was the large living room overlooking the river. This fact was not nearly as important to me as was the stack of *Archie* comic books next to the dusty old couch. A couple of beds were shoved in the single room, and the bathroom . . . well, that was outside.

Just upstream from the property is a little man-made dam that is really just a bunch of rocks stacked up across the river. These rocks give the water something to dance over on the way past the property, creating the most wonderful and constant sound of flowing water. When visiting this sacred space, leave the noise machine at home and just open the window!

That little dam is the perfect spot to cast off on a hot summer day. One day, when I was seven or eight years old, I was on one side of the dam fishing, and my dad was on the opposite side. I hooked into what I assumed was a snag and pulled up on my pole, joking that I had a huge fish on. My dad and I both laughed when suddenly my line went whizzing out from the spool. My snag was moving, and it was big. We locked eyes, which at that point were bugging out of our heads, and Dad went right into coaching mode. I stayed with it and after quite some time had the beast right by the shore.

For any fishing fans reading, I would love to tell you about the huge musky I reeled in, but it was just a large walleye. I got it right up onto the rocks before my line snapped, at which point my father looked as if someone he loved had just died. I looked back at him and yelled, "It's still on the rocks!" With a huge sweeping motion he yelled at me to "grab the son of a bitch." Having no clue as to proper fish-holding technique, I simply reached down with both hands and grabbed the son of a bitch. I left my pole and my tackle box and made the trek back to the shack, dropping that poor fish a half dozen times before reaching my destination. For that entire week I had the opportunity to share my fish story with everyone from grandma and grandpa to aunts and uncles and even to the guy at the local bait shop. This was the first time I ever remember telling a great story, and it is also the first time I ever remember feeling like a hero. Both these feelings were infectious and have not let go of me to this day. All I do is tell stories, and there is nothing I love more than being the hero!

I have so many memories of this place, and they are all incredible, but what marks this sacred space more than anything is not the memories but the river. Not just the river, but the sound it makes. Not just the sound it makes, but the way it moves. In my forty-plus years of existence I have spent countless hours simply staring at and listening to this little section of the Elk River. It connects with me in ways that nothing else in my life does, and I can't truly explain it. If I could do only one thing ever again it would be to sit and look at the Elk River as it moves over that little dam. If I could do two things I would add putting a kayak in the river to feel it under my body.

The Native Priest feels this place and that river so deeply that it has come to define me as a person. Most Native American tribes name their young according to a part of nature that was significant to their family. My name would be Dammed Elk River Kendziera or just Dam Kendziera for short. Recently I was challenged by a spiritual director to consider what part of nature I most resonate with, and I didn't have to think for more than a second. A river! A rushing river! I am a person who is constantly moving and is constantly making noise. (Not literally. I'm actually pretty quiet.) The moment I stop is the moment I become restless, stagnant, and unpleasant to be around. There is peace in movement, and there is unrest in stillness. I love quiet, but I hate stillness. As soon as I accomplish a goal I am looking toward what is next, and I have hundreds of ideas all the time. Most of my ideas are horrible, but they seem monumental when they come to me. I can spend hours of a day laying out a thought or an idea, only to wake up the following day to rip those pages out of my journal after coming up with something even better.

The river in me attracts people, but it also repels them. The reality is that for most, a river is fun for a while, but then it either spits them out or swallows them up. For the longest time I was confused about why so many people would be drawn to me and want to be my friend or to be a part of what I was doing, only to become wildly disappointed or hurt by me. It's because I am a river, and people generally like to stay on the river only for a while before heading to shore. But I am not just the river; I am the rapids flowing over the rocks, which has an even shorter life-span. I am dynamic and exciting, but if you stay with me for too long you might drown. As a person flows with me, a lot of rocks need to be avoided. And even though I move with purpose, I tend to move faster than is comfortable for most. But if you hang in there, the journey will prove exhilarating and will inevitably culminate by entering into a wide expansive ocean with plenty of space to move and explore.

After my parents retired, they tore down the old shack and built a beautiful little house. Even though I was sad to see the shack go, I was at peace. Because it was never about the shack, or the property, but about the river that flows by. This river has continued to flow as I have grown into a man. It has continued to flow as my children have jumped from the dock giggling, growing from infants into young adults. The sound of the river could be heard amid the passion of young budding love and as the background of decades of commitment. It has held me during major life decisions, and it was the soundtrack for the beginning of the book you hold in your hands.

If there is a single place in which the divine resides, it must be on this river. At least for me. And the divine holds other spaces for you. If you came to this little space of the world with me, it is certainly possible that you would be wildly disappointed. You may be disappointed simply because this spot is not your sacred space, and the river may not be a reflection of who you are.

I believe a great disservice religion has brought to our world is the belief that there is a common sacred space for all of us. A space we should all be able to connect with in the same sacred way. I'm not sure there has ever before been such a load of bullshit, and yet many continue to hold it as a truth. I say boldly to religion that you can keep your buildings and your cathedrals. You can keep your rules and your hierarchies. You can keep your beliefs and your guidelines. I choose the river. I choose the divine. I choose myself. Because it is within the truest and most authentic form of myself in which God resides.

Bring It Home

As I have conversations with people who have left organized religion or who are no longer going to church after spending countless Sundays there, one of the first things they often say is that they miss the time of gathering. It had become such a routine that it feels odd when it is gone. I can relate on some level. There is something beautiful, powerful, and meaningful when people gather together for good.

I have heard pastor after pastor share from up front about how the church is not the building, but then when they are met with a person who doesn't enjoy going to church, they go into great detail to explain how immensely important it is for their spiritual wellbeing, which to me sounds like they are saying church does indeed have a lot to do with the building. Don't get me wrong; I live in northern Wisconsin, so I understand the need for a warm, safe space to gather. I just wonder if we could rethink the priority placed on such a space.

When I stopped going to church, it took a little while for me to get used to having a choice about what I wanted to do with my Sunday mornings. I kept saying the "right" thing, which is that I missed it or that I wanted to be a part of a community that meets regularly, but the truth is that was a lie. I actually didn't miss it at all. Not only do I not miss it, but I also kind of love not going anymore. But that is my story, and it does not have to be yours. It's not whether you meet in a building or whether you gather together. What is important is that you have sacred space to connect with God. Mine looks like a small property on a river. It also sometimes looks like a trail in the woods or a country road on my bicycle in the summer. Sometimes it looks like a bonfire with friends or a glass of wine in front of the fireplace with my wife.

Walking toward home will likely require us to walk away from other places that are not a good fit. It is not necessary to leave your church community in order to rethink your faith, but much of the time that does seem to be the case. All my life I have known where the sacred spaces in my life were. Yet I was foolish enough for many years to let others convince me I was wrong. In the end, the church building is no longer standing in my life, yet that little dam on the Elk River remains. Find your sacred spaces—the places that inspire you and give perspective, the places where everything makes sense even for just a few moments. When you find these spaces, spend as much time there as you can.

6

Imperfection

Perfection is not attainable, but if we chase
perfection we can catch excellence.

—Vince Lombardi

FOR THE STORY IN THIS chapter to have its full impact, it will be
important to visualize the home and property I grew up on. As I
mentioned earlier, we lived a few miles outside of town. I like to say
that we lived in the middle of nowhere outside of the middle of
nowhere. The Wisconsin River flows through much of Wisconsin,
cutting through my hometown about twenty miles before reaching
the Mississippi, and on both sides are beautiful rolling bluffs. Our
home was halfway up one of these bluffs, off a gravel road. The
grade of the hill was significant enough that on many cold, snowy
mornings we had to hike down to the bottom to meet the school
bus, which was incapable of climbing the slope. Our home was on
seventeen acres of this hillside, and our backyard was a steep incline
that was difficult to walk up without using the leverage of small
trees to pull on. The house had a deck on three sides and was full of
windows, bringing lovely natural light in throughout the entire day.

My mother is a wonderfully strong and independent woman to
whom I attribute most of my respect for women. She isn't strong in

terms of being strict or stern; quite the opposite. Mom was and is very laid-back. She takes life as it comes, unless she doesn't like a particular president in office, in which case she suddenly gets extremely opinionated. She is strong and independent in a way that a person would need to be to climb the hill behind the house in the snow to cut down a Christmas tree and drag it back down while dad was at work and we were at school. When we left, there was no tree in the house, and when we got home, there was. She is strong and independent in the way you need to be to put in twenty miles on a bicycle many days before waking us up for school at 6:00 a.m. And speaking of biking, she is strong and independent in the way that, after her youngest son proudly shared a picture of his bicycle odometer after hitting 1,000 miles for the season, sent back a picture of her odometer reading 1,500 miles. And this was when she was in her sixties. The woman takes a bike ride each year on her birthday equaling the same mileage as the age she is turning. I won't give away her exact age, but I am in my midforties; feel free to do some general calculations.

In addition to being strong and independent, she also is a great lover of nature, which is mildly surprising since she grew up in Milwaukee. I am guessing this came from my grandfather, who was known for being able to identify most birds from their songs and lived on the lake in his little aluminum boat for most of the fishing season. She was composting before it was the trendy hipster thing to do and was concerned about healthy eating before all the conversations about preservatives and sugar became a craze.

We had two cats growing up. My parents made the mistake of letting their boys name them during the height of our Kid 'n Play and DJ Jazzy Jeff & the Fresh Prince phase, and we lovingly welcomed our new kittens, Funky and Dude, into the family. Funky and Dude, like their owners, were indoor-outdoor beings, spending equal amounts of time in both spaces. We had crank-open windows in our living room, and my mom decided that it was easier to let the cats in the window instead of the door. I guess this was the one part of her life where she was a bit lazy; you could open the window without leaving the comfort of your chair. Anytime the cats wanted to come in, they simply came to the window, we opened it, and they hopped in.

There was one problem with this arrangement. The problem was that these cats loved being outside in the country because they spent their days hunting for mice, moles, and chipmunks. They were truly living the cat dream. Unfortunately for Dude, one day that dream must have become a nightmare as he left and never returned. It's fair to say that the hunter became the hunted, but I digress. Cats like to show off their trophy dead animals. I guess in some ways they are not all that different from humans who like to hang dead things on their walls. Because of this we were taught that when the cats tapped on the window wanting to come in, we were required to have a visual on their mouths to make sure that weren't coming home for a little show-and-tell time. As soon as we verified that there were no dead animals, we could crank open the window and let them in.

In general, my mom is a very perceptive person who is well aware of her surroundings. The woman tends to have her shit together. But we all have our moments, and on one fateful day that moment came in our living room by the crank window when the cat wanted to come in. Funky came home and did his normal routine. My mom heard him and, in a moment of distraction, forgot the most important step in this cat dance. She didn't remember to check the cat's mouth for an animal. Funky seized the opportunity and without hesitating hopped into the house with his latest catch, which in this case was a chipmunk.

My mom immediately realized her mistake and jumped into action. Best-case scenario, the chipmunk was dead, so she just had to get the cat to drop it and dispose of it in the woods. No big deal. This, however, was not the best-case scenario: the chipmunk was still alive. I have not received verbal confirmation from my mom on this next part, but I am fairly confident that when she realized that the animal was still alive, a hero song began playing in her head. Maybe it was the theme song to *Rocky*, *Magnum PI*, or *The Golden Girls*, but whatever it was, I believe it was the motivating soundtrack for her mission in life at that moment.

Step one was to separate Funky from his prize catch. Mom was able to spook him enough to cause him to drop the little guy (or girl), and she quickly closed Funky in the bathroom. She then gazed over at the chipmunk lying on the floor. I don't really know how to explain the poor little rodent's condition other than to say that the chipmunk was not dead but was also really not all that alive either. His life was most certainly hanging in the balance. Right or wrong, mom's perspective was that the best chance of survival for the chipmunk was to return him to his natural environment. I don't want to doubt her judgment, but I would think returning it to the woods would simply give another animal a shot at a decent lunch, but it wasn't my call, so I'll keep my two cents to myself.

As the theme song played in her mind, I also think I recall a light from heaven shining down upon her as God was recognizing her good deed of taking care of this poor little creature. Although it is certainly possible that it was just a coincidence and that the sun was shining through the window at a convenient time. It's also quite possible that I have made all this up in my head because again, the truth is I wasn't even home when this happened, and I am simply regurgitating what I remember mom telling me and inserting a lot of my boyish wonder.

Mom went into the laundry room and grabbed a dustpan. She returned to her miniature patient and gently scooped him up. He was going to be safe now! As her hero song continued on repeat in her head, she exited the back patio door with a plan of walking up the steep hill behind our house to a safe place far away from Funky the cat. The problem with doing a good deed like this is that it is easy to get lost in the moment. As my mother was walking up the steep slope, she was leaning forward for balance and lost track of the task at hand. As she leaned forward, she accidentally tipped the dustpan slightly forward. The little rodent slowly slid off the dustpan and onto the ground in front of my dear mother, and because of the song, the light, the steep hill, or simply a lapse in focus, she did not realize what had happened until with her next stride she stepped on that poor little chipmunk that had fallen in front of her. As my mother lifted up her foot, she saw the little being lying there. And whatever part of that chipmunk that was alive upon leaving the house was now most certainly gone. The save-the-chipmunk campaign suddenly turned into a bury-the-chipmunk ceremony.

Bring It Home

As we journey back home, we will find that our failures sometimes define us. They define us as human beings, incapable of perfection. Incapable of living up to the bar. Incapable of being a good Christian. And as we find peace in the midst of our constant screwups, we will undoubtedly find humility. Where humility is found, that is also the place where we are most likely to find a divine presence. If you keep screwing up in the same way over and over like I do, you will find God there over and over. And here is the best news: your life is your life. Your faith journey is yours and yours alone. Because of that, we can be free to succeed and fail on our own terms. And we don't have to give anyone the authority to hold anything over our heads.

Arguably one of the biggest challenges with most religions, and certainly Christianity, is that we feel this constant need to live up to expectations or to "live above reproach" (Titus 1:6–9). I've got to be honest. I feel that most of my life is lived well below reproach, and I'm not even fully confident that I know what *reproach* means. If you have ever been in any sort of leadership role in a church or a faith-based organization, you know those expectations can be absolutely suffocating.

After being in leadership together for nearly two decades, my wife and I have had to work really hard to discover what is actually true and authentic about our relationship because we spent so much time trying to act like the perfect Christian married couple. And it has been extremely difficult on us. After giving hundreds upon hundreds of messages and sermons about the "truth," and after so many years of the modern church machine using me and attempting to form me into its image, I am now in the challenging space of discovering what the truth about myself is.

Most of us set the bar high in our lives. We want to be great at our careers, great in our relationships, great parents, and so on. But just like my mom, as we try to be the hero, we mess up all the time and end up killing the very thing we were trying to save. We ruin relationships, care more about ourselves than others, cheat, lie, lust, and hate. And when we do these things, we do not become unqualified for a relationship with the divine. We actually become more available to it.

When I was in college, we were having an all-night jazz band rehearsal before heading out on tour. In the middle of the rehearsal our instructor pulled out the next tune and set it on his music stand. He scanned the room and said, "Your goal on this next tune is to play it perfectly without a single mistake." As he said this, he held a conducting baton horizontally above his head. He then continued, "None of you are capable of doing this. But if you shoot for perfection and fail, you will always do better than if you shoot for mediocrity and succeed."

Set your bar as high as you desire. Shoot for it each and every day. Fail each and every day. And as you do, expect to find God there.

7
Pride

A proud man is always looking down on things and people;
and, of course, as long as you are looking down,
you cannot see something that is above you.

—C. S. Lewis

MY EARLY CAREER OPTIONS OF being a Catholic priest and a Native American fell by the wayside by the time I was in second or third grade, which left me grasping for a new future. I recall completing a questionnaire about career choices in grade school, and the best option for me came up as an orthodontist. I don't know what questions I answered to bring about that conclusion, but the idea of a life of looking into people's mouths for forty hours a week was an absolute no-go for me, so I was still at ground zero in my search.

And then it happened! I went to a show at the high school gymnasium featuring a group called the Kids from Wisconsin. It was a big group of teenagers who were singing and dancing with a full twelve-piece band, and I was simply enthralled! I didn't care much for the singing and could take or leave the dancing, but the band! About halfway through the second half there was a song that featured the drummer, who just happened to be a local student. The band reached a frenzied crescendo before cutting off and leaving the stage. All of them, that is, except the drummer. His hands moved effortlessly around the set, making sounds that I had never in my life heard before.

After exhausting the options in front of him, he proceeded to get up from behind the drum set and move around the stage, turning everything he encountered into a percussion instrument. After showing off his technique and speed right in front of the cheering audience, he made his way back behind the drums and suddenly stopped. He grabbed a towel, wiped off his forehead in true showman form, and slowly and deliberately started what sounded to me like a train leaving the station. His speed gradually increased until he was just a flurry of arms flying around, drums and cymbals clanging and banging in harmony, creating a sound that was screaming my name. The band suddenly appeared back onstage, and the drummer yelled at the top of his lungs, "One! Two! One, two, three, four!" And the band came screaming in to end the tune. When the final note sounded, the room erupted in applause as the star came forward for a bow. I pointed at him and said, "That is what I am going to do for the rest of my life!"

Later that evening, I told my parents that I wanted to be a drummer, and in an act that has defined my life, my career, and even my parenting, they said, "That sounds like a great idea." They bought me a Fraggle Rock toy drum set for Christmas that year, which I demolished, putting holes in every drum within a matter of days. Then I told them I actually needed a real drum set. Dad grabbed the newspaper classifieds, which for you young folks was the precursor to eBay and Facebook Marketplace, and within a week I had a sparkly red Rogers drum set. In a stroke of good fortune, the drummer I'd seen onstage was a member of a family that attended our church, and as if the universe couldn't be more obvious, my mom worked for his

dad, who was the town lawyer. Not only did I get a sparkly red drum
set, but I also got set up with weekly lessons with none other than
Stan Slamen, the famous Kids from Wisconsin drummer. I had one
goal and one goal only: to become a Kids from Wisconsin drummer!
This was a goal he and I shared for me, and Stan proceeded to kick
my ass every single week trying to impart his wisdom and ability to
his new protégé.

One of the strange gifts I am blessed with is that all my limbs can
operate independently of each other. You know the old thing where
you pat your head and rub your tummy in a circle? No problem for
this guy. I could pat my head and rub my tummy. I could change the
direction in which I was rubbing my tummy, and then I could rub
my head and pat my tummy. Like I said, a true protégé. At school I
treated my pencils like drumsticks to control the fidgeting I inherited from my mother, whose leg constantly bounces to this day. My
teacher would call me out in front of the whole class and say, "Matt,
please stop. We all know you are a drummer." All I heard was, "Matt
. . . you are a drummer!" To this day I keep drum sticks nearby when
I am podcasting or writing for those times I get fidgety. As I write
this, there is a pair right next to me that my teenage kids bought me
as a Christmas gift.

I practiced my ass off because I knew if I didn't, I would be
blasted and shamed at my next lesson. In general I am against sham-
ing, but it was like magic for my development as a drummer. We
started with rock music, which led me to bands like Living Colour,
Led Zeppelin, and Metallica. I would practice for hours and hours
each day trying to perfect every song I was inspired by. Then I was
introduced to Buddy Rich, and my life changed forever. If you have
never heard of him, do a quick Google search and let your mind be
blown! Buddy Rich was one of the greatest jazz drummers ever and

was also known for being one of the biggest assholes the music industry has ever known, firing band members after screaming at them on the tour bus and forcing the bus driver to stop in the middle of nowhere to kick the musician in question out the door. Buddy Rich was my gateway drug to jazz music, and I have never gone back!

I learned big band, swing, bebop, and then Latin beats like the samba and bossa nova that made me wish I was from somewhere far south of Wisconsin. All this practicing was rewarded when I became the youngest person ever to be accepted into the Kids from Wisconsin. I traveled with the group for four years before getting a scholarship and attending the University of Wisconsin Eau Claire, where I performed with the *DownBeat*-award-winning and Grammy-nominated Jazz Ensemble I. This led to a stint at Disney World and the opportunity to play with many of the people I would practice along with in my bedroom growing up.

This type of focus, intentionality, and drive came with a price tag. You know the old story about the man who sold his soul to the devil to become a great blues guitar player? There is some truth to that story, because you have to have a certain type of mindset to land an audition or to play with the best. For me that was a deep-seated pridefulness I still struggle with to this day. My teacher told me I had to walk into every room and every audition believing I was the best. And that is exactly what I did. When people would compliment me on a performance, on the outside I would say, "Thank you," but on the inside I would think, *I know.*

This has poured into every aspect of my life over the years. When I played in a Christian band where we were supposed to be "leading people to the Lord," all I really cared about was being the best. And the world—especially the Christian world—was happy to encourage me in this endeavor as I continued to receive accolades well into adulthood.

Eventually I got pretty bored with drumming (chalk it up to being an Enneagram seven) and stumbled upon something else I was good at, which is speaking in front of people. As soon as I figured out I was good, I studied my ass off to become great. And when I had opportunities—you guessed it—I wanted to be the absolute best. I relished the reality that when I spoke at our church, more people ordered CDs of the sermon than when the lead pastor spoke. I grinned from ear to ear when camp directors told me I was the highest-rated speaker in a given year, and when people would say I should be a national speaker, on the outside I would say, "Thank you," while on the inside I would think, *Of course I should.*

The universe is a great teacher, and sin has very natural consequences. It turns out there are a lot of places in life where being the best doesn't fly. That mentality does not work in a marriage. It doesn't work in parenting. It doesn't work in friendships. And it doesn't work when trying to address justice issues in our world. In these spaces, and in many others, what matters is character, integrity, trust, and confidence.

As we get older, if we are in authentic spaces with honest people, they will be happy to call out our cockiness because the older and wiser we get, the less becoming pride is. In the past six months alone I have had three people I care for and respect a great deal call me out on my arrogance. On the outside I said, "Thank you," and on the inside I say, *I know.*

My problem seems to be a problem we have in our world as a whole. When I was in the inner circles of the church, the most common question I would hear among pastors was, "How many people attend your church?" They did and still do elevate leaders to superstar status. And during all this time spent caring about shit that doesn't matter, people are feeling alone, people are being left out, and people are leaving in droves. The numbers religious leaders care so much about will continue to decrease as people continue to see through the facade. Being the best won't feel so great when pastors are preaching to empty seats. Just ask the leaders of virtually every mainline denomination in the world today.

In the political arena we continue to vote based on what will help us the most, dismissing the interests of others who might be in a different situation in life. We hold up those who fight for what we want as if they are some sort of savior, waving flags and packing auditoriums. We scream at each other and put out belittling posts online because, of course, we know the truth. We know what is right, and if you are on the other side, well, you simply do not know right from wrong. I don't believe in an actual hell, but if I did, this attitude would be straight from the pit of it. And where has this attitude gotten us? Here. Look around. Things are not looking very good. And too often we play the God card to back our opinions in order to help us feel okay with our ugly, world-destroying sin.

There is a passage in the Bible where Paul, who was as prideful as they come, was talking about Jesus and described him as one who did not consider equality with God something to be grasped (Philippians 2:6). The concept is that if God and Jesus are one or are on the same plane, Jesus willingly chose not to give a shit about it. Instead he took on the very nature of a servant, only caring about things that actually matter.

Should we try to excel in life and be the best with what we have? Only to the degree to which we can use it to help those around us. Selling the most books, having the biggest following, or having the most money is fleeting. Just ask someone who has any of these things. If they are honest, they will tell you that sometimes a blessing is a curse and sometimes a curse is a blessing.

I once worked for a church in a very wealthy suburb of Minneapolis, and one of the staff members there also worked as a chaplain for the police department. He responded to a suicide call one day and was surprised when he pulled up to a huge house in an affluent neighborhood. The police and paramedics were all gathered in the garage. As he made his way to the garage, he saw a woman lying lifeless on the ground next to her new Jaguar. After they removed the body, the police looked closely at the tire of the vehicle. When my coworker got closer, he noticed that there were lipstick prints on the tire. This woman drove her car into the garage and closed the door while leaving the car running. She lied down next to it and kissed the tire before breathing her final breath on this earth. Everything she worked for left her with a love for something incapable of loving her back. Her quest for the most and the best left her lonely, shattered, and dead.

That story is the story of our world. In our quest to be the best, the most successful, the richest, or the most liked, we end up lifeless. True life and true happiness are not found in our greatness but in our smallness. They are found in conversations with friends, in the eyes of our children, in the causes of the oppressed, and in the hearts of the humble.

I sit with my drumsticks by my side. They now serve two purposes. First, as I already mentioned, they keep me from fidgeting so much. Second, and more importantly, they remind me of a person I don't want to be and a place I don't want to return to. Do I want this book to sell a bunch of copies? Do I want to gain some traction and attention? Yes, yes I do. But only if it will help those who read it, and only if I can do it without needing to be the best. I pray this book is simply one in a sea of books, songs, movies, and art that changes lives and changes hearts. I simply hope that it finds its space in this big world that has plenty of room for all of us.

Bring It Home

The path of faith deconstruction is strewn with a bunch of arrogant human beings. I can say that confidently because, as in most areas of my existence, when I think I know something, I naturally get prideful about it. When I refer to the arrogant human beings, I willingly include myself as a part of that group.

A horrible reality in life is that we too often become what we hate. The abused often become abusers. Kids of alcoholics often become alcoholics. Former Evangelicals who had "truth" wielded over them now wield their new version of "truth" over everyone. My greatest fear is that up from the ashes of Evangelicalism will rise just another shitty version of religious nonsense led by arrogant know-it-alls.

My greatest hope is that we will learn from the mistakes of others and also from mistakes we have made. My hope is that we will assume we are still going to get it wrong because, after all, we are talking about a great divine mystery. And this great mystery has no conclusion. The divine is not some sort of riddle to be solved, but a great wonder to be experienced.

Pride is fragility wrapped in a pretty package. I need to be the best and be right so I don't have to deal with the reality that I am actually neither. As you find faith again, don't forget that most of us thought we had a corner on the truth not that long ago. It turns out those corners were more rounded than we thought.

8

Grace

I don't deserve this award, but I have arthritis and
I don't deserve that either.

—Jack Benny

WE OFTEN HEAR PEOPLE TALK about love at first sight, which is a beautiful sentiment, but when I met my Suzie, it was love at first sound.

I was sixteen years old and part of a performing group I mentioned in the previous chapter, the Kids from Wisconsin. The organization chartered a bus to get the group from town to town, and our parents entrusted the leaders of this organization with keeping track of us. So each time we got on the bus, we had to count off based on our assigned numbers; if the numbers one to thirty-three were all called out, everyone was accounted for. I was young and was in the band, which naturally meant that I sat near the front of the bus because everyone knows the cool kids sit in the back.

Suzie is a couple years older than me and is an incredible singer and an extrovert whom everyone wants to be friends with, which, as you can imagine, garnered her a seat in the back. It was the first official count-off of the year since we were getting ready for our first performance. This was my second year with the group, so I knew the routine. When the counting began, everything seemed normal until suddenly this low, raspy, sexy voice called out her number, and it felt as if the universe began to move in slow motion. My heart began to pound through my chest as I slowly turned about to see where this heavenly sound was coming from. I soon recognized the infectious presence of none other than Suzanne Peloquin.

At this point my heart quickly dropped, and time went back to normal. I was well aware that this woman was so far out of my league that even daydreaming about being with her seemed ridiculous. And, just to be clear, I am not being self-deprecating in any way; sometimes it just is what it is, and it is important to understand your place in the world. My place in the world and Suzanne's place in the world were in two different zip codes. And although I am guessing she would refute this, for the entire summer I only remember her talking to me one time. To make things even worse, that one time was when I, along with another band member, picked her up at her boyfriend's house to take them to the bus. That is the definition of demoralizing.

I tried to get Suzie out of my mind, but I couldn't. Every time I saw her or heard that raspy voice (which was that way because she sang too much and had vocal nodules, which are callouses on the vocal cords) or even just thought about her, I would daydream of what it would be like if she were mine. In a grand stroke of luck we ended up going to the same college a couple years later. I had no idea this was the case until, on my first day there, I was walking across the footbridge that connected two sides of the campus after my music theory class, and I passed her as she walked the other way. She was always with friends and never noticed me, but on this glorious day she was by herself. Our eyes met, and she said . . . "Hi." I was with a new friend at the time, and after this happened, he looked at me with a grin on his face and said, "She's gorgeous. How do you know her?"

There were plenty of times that semester when I did not need to cross the bridge after my class, but I put on my coat and crossed it anyway because I knew I would get to see Suzie and she just might say hello.

At this point in the story, it is fair to say that my obsession with Suzie was getting a little unhealthy. But at the same time, it seemed as if the universe kept allowing me to run into her. Granted, I did my best to help the universe out as best I could by sitting next to her when I saw her alone at Catholic mass or by trying to wish away her boyfriend, whom I knew could never be as good for her as I could be. But I would see her everywhere. And every time I saw her, I would think about what it would be like to hold her hand or kiss her or even just have a conversation with her. But, as I have already mentioned, she was and still is to this day well out of my league.

The summer after my freshman year of college, I jumped on board for a final time with the same summer performing group I met Suzanne in. She had long since moved on to bigger and better things. At the end of the summer, the Kids from Wisconsin would go to Florida, where the producer and founder was from, to do a week of shows at retirement communities. When we were not performing, we got to spend the days at the beach, which we all took advantage of every single day. Now, even though I am as white as can be, if I spend enough time out in the sun I actually get pretty dark. So much that one summer later in my college years I was working as a landscaper, and someone at my church got very excited because there was a Latino man going to their church. Diversity in Eau Claire, Wisconsin, gets people excited. To their grand disappointment, I turned around during the greeting time, and they realized it was just me.

When the bus got back from Florida that year, I drove straight to college since I was already a few days late for the beginning of the semester. As I was beginning to mature, the realization that Suzanne was likely not a part of my future had begun to sink in, and I started dating someone else who was in nearly every way the opposite of Suzie.

When I got back to school, I needed to do a little catching up, especially in my music history class. Part of that infamous class was that we had to be able to listen to classical music and identify the composer, name of the piece, and time period it was from. This was well before the days of digital music, so we had to listen to tapes and CDs. College students don't generally have enough money to buy hundreds of recordings, so the school offered a room called the listening lab. It was basically a library of music where you could sit and listen to free of charge. So on my first day back at the university, at the beginning of my sophomore year, a moment happened that changed my life forever. If I were to judge moments from most important to least important, this one would be at the very top—no doubt about it. On one side of the listening lab door was life before, and on the other side was life after. I walked down the hall, grabbed the door handle, turned it, and pushed the door open. I immediately looked to my right, seeing the newest employee of the music department listening lab was none other than Suzanne Peloquin. My heart leaped out of my chest, and my knees buckled a bit as our eyes met. And in the same low, raspy, sexy voice that I heard for the first time more than three years earlier, the woman I had been infatuated with for that entire time, the woman of my dreams who was so far outside of my league that we were arguably in different sports altogether, said, and I quote, "Matt, wow, you look really hot. Do you have a girlfriend?" This is not me trying to be funny. This is not me exaggerating. I let her read this before sending it to my publisher, and those, my friends, were her exact words!

Now, to be fair, since the time we first met I had grown up a lot. There is a big difference between a sixteen-year-old and a nineteen-year-old. I got my braces off, graduated from high school, and, let's not forget, was sporting a pretty nice tan. Also, to be fair, Suzie is one of the boldest humans I know, and she also loves to have fun, so a portion of what she said was her being coy. I choose to believe that she was mostly serious, but we could debate that all day long. The best part about this story is that the woman of my dreams told me I was hot and asked if I had a girlfriend. The horrible part about this story is that I did. But, as if the universe couldn't be any more obvious, that girlfriend's car broke down the following weekend before she was supposed to come visit me. Not wanting to miss an obvious opportunity to swing for the fences and go after a dream, I asked Suzie if she was going to the evening's gala concert, and when she confirmed, I asked if she would like to go with me, which she also confirmed. After the concert we went to a local coffee shop and enjoyed some great music before heading back to her place. We talked for hours until falling asleep lying on her bed. So if you want to know if we slept together after our first date, the answer is yes, in the most literal sense. I woke up the next morning and headed back to my dorm feeling like I was walking on a cloud. I walked in the door of my room, picked up the phone, and let my girlfriend know that it wasn't going to work.

I was so excited that I skipped over the part where I was supposed to ask Suzie if she wanted to date me and simply told her that we were indeed dating. I shared the news with some of my best friends, and, I kid you not, they laughed at me because they actually thought I was joking. This is how far out of my league this woman was. Weeks later one of them, after seeing her perform, looked at me and said, "I still can't believe you are dating her."

From that time forward we spent every possible moment with each other. Less than a year later Suzie moved to New York City to study with a Broadway vocal coach. Our dream was that she would be onstage and I would be in the orchestra pit. She would most certainly have held up her end of the bargain but decided that living in a big city and working six days a week wasn't all it's cracked up to be. I am no idiot and am well aware that I would not be the only guy interested in such a beautiful, talented, and outgoing woman, so when she headed to New York City, I headed to the ring store.

Suzie came to see me over Christmas. I had it all planned out. After she came to watch me play a jazz gig, we were going to go on a nice winter hike to a nearby park where some friends of ours had set up flowers on a bench and had "The Christmas Song" by Nat King Cole playing on a boom box on repeat. Just to be clear, "playing on repeat" at that time in history meant recording the song over and over again on a tape cassette so it would play for thirty minutes straight. Also, I can't remember which was more expensive: the ring or the batteries for the boom box. Six C-size batteries is tough on a college kid's bank account. The only problem with my little scheme was that old man winter must not be a romantic, because it was nearly twenty degrees below zero that evening. Again, I am not exaggerating. So when I asked Suzie to go on a little stroll with me, she kindly, but very directly, declined. Thankfully after my second request she gave in. We walked two blocks over to the park, and as we approached the bench, she could hear the music. She sat, I knelt, I asked, and she tackled me in the snow. Although she never actually said "yes," I'm pretty sure that counts.

I tried my hardest to honor my parents by waiting until after college to get married, but after another year of being apart and racking up hefty phone bills, it all felt a bit ridiculous, so we just went ahead and got married ahead of schedule. It was a big Catholic wedding that felt more like a two-hour concert since we had all our music friends perform. The priest did a sermon that included the word *prostitute* no less than three times—again, not joking. And by the end we were married.

From a sexy voice in the back of the bus, to a borderline unhealthy obsession, to a suntan and a coy comment, to a broken-down vehicle and an explosive connection, I was a married man before I was a college graduate. And more than two decades later, through all the ups and downs of life, career, kids, and relationship, her voice has healed up and is no longer so raspy—but I still have a pretty unhealthy obsession. We like to say that we want our kisses to make our kids mildly uncomfortable, and they most certainly do.

Bring It Home

When we look back over our faith journey, it can often feel like an unhealthy relationship involving broken promises, abuse, and a nasty breakup. But if there is a God out there who loves us and desires the best for us, shouldn't it feel more like an exciting obsession than an abusive relationship?

As you head back home, I hope you see the divine everywhere you go. And I hope when you do that those moments make your heart leap with excitement. It seems odd to settle when we have the option to swing for the fences. We may not feel like we deserve it, and we may not feel like we are worth something so special and amazing. But we might as well try, because you just never know.

9

Being Good Enough

You'll never do a whole lot unless you're brave enough to try.
—Dolly Parton

SHORTLY AFTER MOVING TO BOSCOBEL, my father began the daunting journey of building our family home. He bought a kit, the company dropped it off on the property, and he grabbed his tool belt and got to work. In a world in which we bitch and moan about having to assemble the Ikea furniture we purchased, my father had a house dropped off in pieces and put it together with his sheer willpower and a hammer. He didn't have a nail gun with a compressor. The man had a hammer and a pocketful of nails. He built a beautiful home that would hold many memories for a family at the beginning of their grand adventure.

To give you a clear picture of my family, there's my father, a self-trained engineer capable of pretty much anything he puts his mind to. There's my mother, who, again, would cut down Christmas trees on our property and drag them into our house by herself. Then my older brother, who has a brilliant mechanical mind which he currently uses to build high-end bicycles for a living. And then there is this strange, unique boy who came into the world with a lovely, sensitive heart, a love for music, abnormally good rhythm, and a heart for the oppressed. Cue the song "One of These Things Is Not Like the Other" here!

One quality I have always possessed, likely inspired by my dad, is a belief that I can do anything I put my mind to. I also don't consider failure an option and have enough optimism to believe that everything is going to turn out okay in the end. And let's not forget about my unmatched levels of stubbornness and cockiness. What I lack in ability, I make up for in belief!

In the back of my mind, I always wondered, *What if I could build a house like my dad did?* I was so impressed and inspired by the feat he pulled off almost single-handedly—not just once with the house I grew up in, but a second time after tearing down the old shack on the river—that in spite of my complete lack of construction skills, I believed my lot in life included building a house. Just to be clear on how ridiculous this idea was, not only did I lack knowledge, I did not even own a tool belt.

Fast-forward a number of years, and I was a young husband and father. My wife and I had an infant daughter and were convinced another was not too far behind. At the time we lived in an adorable old story-and-a-half house right in town. Then it happened! I had the thought, and I somehow let it slip out of my mouth one night as I said, "We should look for land and build a house." Once those words were out, I certainly couldn't take them back! And before I knew it we were on the hunt for land out in the country.

When I said, "We should build a house," I did not mean we should approve some plans and let someone else build the house. Often people say they are building a house when in fact they are paying someone else to build a house for them. This was not what I had in mind. I was going to build a house like my dad built a house. Strap on a tool belt and build it from the ground up. If a house was going to be built, damn it, I was going to be the one swinging the hammer. To be fair, I did buy a nice framing nailer, but the concept still applies.

Within a couple of months my wife Suzie and I located some property, bought it, and began working on the design. The drummer and dreamer committed to building an actual house. And, my friends, that is what I did! I did have to recruit my dad, who actually knew what he was doing. He started with a trip to the local hardware store to buy his son a tool belt. Then he came up every weekend. We'd work together all weekend, and before he'd go he'd give me a list of assignments to complete before he returned. That is the routine we followed for nearly nine months. I built a house with my soft musician hands and a brain that is incapable of understanding the simplest of electrical concepts. By Christmas I moved my pregnant wife and two-year-old daughter into a really spectacular three-bedroom home, a home that would hold memories and create the foundation of who we would become.

We live in a world that promotes safety and security but ultimately rewards belief and risk. Recently I met a man at a local establishment, and when I asked him what he did for a living, he began in a fashion that seemed as if he wanted to impress me. He shared the details and intricacy of the work he did to pay his mortgage and support his family. Then something fascinating happened. He bluntly stopped mid-sentence, looked me in the eye, and said, "I hate my fucking job." I then asked what he would love to do, and he didn't have to think twice about it. He knew without a doubt that he wanted to be a fishing and hunting guide. After sharing his dream for a few minutes, he quickly backtracked and shared that he would never attempt to go after his true desire. He had a plethora of excuses for why it wouldn't work, so he decided not to try.

Just because we don't own a tool belt doesn't mean we can't build a house. Just because we can't see a way doesn't mean a way doesn't exist. The beginning lies in the decision. Once I decided to build the house, it became a foregone conclusion. And once the hole was dug for the basement, there was no going back. It was the most difficult thing I have ever done in my entire life. I was sore every single day. I bled all over that house. At one point I stapled my hand to the roof. I had more moments of doubt than you could ever imagine. I released more swear words in nine months than in my entire life to that point. But in the end, there was a house. An actual house that humans could live in.

We can take this concept and apply it to many areas of life. But at the end of the day, the point is to reject this culture's belief that you have to know what you are doing before you try. We have to reject the idea that there is a set path to reach each destination. I was a builder without a tool belt. I have been a pastor without a seminary degree. I am an introvert who has created a career as a public speaker. And I am a human who believes there is better in this world than shitty religious constructs, hateful ideologies, and propaganda meant to keep us all in line.

After living in that house for ten years, it happened again. I started focusing all my attention on all of the negatives. In the house I built, the frame of the kitchen window was directly in the way of the view to the back yard. In the house I built, there was a huge crack in the drywall because the wall face above the hallway was too big. In the house I built, the fireplace was not energy efficient. What if I tried again? And that is exactly what I did. As I write this chapter, I am sitting in the second house I built. The soft, sensitive musician boy built not one but two homes, and the second one he and his equally determined and driven wife pretty much pulled off on their own. There is very little that brings me more joy than when someone enters our house, hears that we built it, and asks, "Do you mean that you actually built it?" To which I respond with a smirk on my face, "Yes—yes we did!"

Bring It Home

One reality that exists in all people is our struggle to believe we are good enough, smart enough, strong enough, or holy enough. The religious system presented to many of us is one in which we are told there is a person on top who has more understanding about God than the rest of us. Because they were afforded the opportunity to be indoctrinated by a Bible college or seminary, they now have some sort of inside track, causing the rest of us to feel a level of inferiority.

The truth is that none of that matters. A friend of mine once shared with me that the biggest spiritual influence in his life was his illiterate mother. She was incapable of reading the Bible yet understood Jesus on a deeper level than any other person he had ever met.

On your journey back home, when you feel inferior and think you cannot possibly understand God, know that you are correct because God is not meant to be understood that way. Our faith journey is not about retaining certainty; it is about wonder. It is not about complete understanding; it is about accepting mystery.

Friends, I have a music education degree from a state school in Wisconsin. I have never been to a single Bible class. There is no theology or seminary degree hanging on any of my walls, and there are no initials behind my name. You can be sure that reality has caused me a good deal of self-doubt. I struggle to understand how I was invited to speak to tens of thousands of young people over the years.

I am confused at how it was possible to be called chaplain and asked to give spiritual advice to inmates for seven years of my life. And I cannot comprehend how on earth it was possible for people to consider me their pastor for nearly a decade. It wasn't because of my great knowledge of the Bible or because of my vast education. It was because I wasn't afraid to take risks. I simply went where I felt I should go and did what I thought I should do. I also do not have a contractor's license, yet both the houses I built are still standing.

During your spiritual pilgrimage, don't let your lack of understanding, knowledge, or education get in the way of your ability to find God or experience the divine. If this was about knowing the right answers, maybe a degree would be helpful. But as my friend Colby Martin stated during an interview for my podcast, "If a good teacher is to get a student to get the right answers on a test, and if Jesus was supposed to get us to get the right answers for when we die, then can we just be honest and say, 'not a good teacher.'"

We all lack understanding. We all lack clarity. We all lack knowledge. And maybe that is the point. As a carpenter, Jesus was certainly more qualified to build a house than I am. But he, like myself and like most of you, was wildly underqualified for any position of spiritual authority. It appears we are in good company.

10

Don't Kill Me

We are made for goodness. We are made for love. . . . We are
made for all of the beautiful things that you and I know.
We are made to tell the world that there are no outsiders.
All, all are welcome.

—Desmond Tutu

I REMEMBER GROWING UP HEARING stories during history class
about the bombing of Pearl Harbor. It was a terrible moment in
American history when people from across the globe had the audac-
ity to come attack America. The narrative quickly surfaced that
people of Japanese descent were to be feared because if one is capable, they are all capable. This cost thousands of American citizens
their livelihoods and their ability to live peacefully in the "Land of
the Free." The full circle occurred when thousands of innocent Japanese citizens were mercilessly wiped from the planet by two bomb-
ings that will haunt us forever.

Fast-forward several decades, and I was on a phone call with a
contact for an event booking when the man soberly asked me if my
television was on. I informed him that it was not, and he simply told
me to turn it on and we could pick up our conversation another time.
I turned on the TV and within a matter of minutes saw the first of

the two World Trade Center towers crash to the ground. I was watching in real time something that looked as if it was happening in a movie. Just a short time later the second tower came down, and the country entered into a corporate sense of shock. *What happened? How did it happen? Are we safe? Will it happen again?* Images quickly began flooding out from the horrible events, and within a very short time we were made aware that this was a terrorist attack from extremist Muslim men in the name of Allah.

They say that history repeats itself, and I would simply respond, "Only if we don't learn from it." What we did not learn from Pearl Harbor is that a small group of people do not represent the whole. Instead, we once again villainized an entire people group and used military power to offer a false sense of security. Within a very short time hate crimes against Muslims were a regular occurrence. Mosques were being vandalized and destroyed, and many realized religious freedom in our country had a huge asterisk next to it.

Faith leaders were quick to jump on the bandwagon, pulling out portions of the Koran that appeared to promote an idea that to adhere to the Muslim faith, there was a need to hate and kill people of other faiths, especially Christians. These loud, prominent voices left many Christians feeling a sense of fear anytime they would see someone from the Middle East. I could easily pull out several verses from the Old Testament of "The Word of God" that seemingly make it clear that for Christianity to move forward, military power and wiping groups of people from the face of the earth who believed differently is the way to go. This is a proverbial pot-calling-the-kettle-black scenario. The full circle happened as the US once again used military dominance and propaganda to conquer and kill many terrorists along with thousands of innocent civilians. Everyone cheered and once again felt a wonderful but false sense of safety and security as the president stood on an aircraft carrier foolishly claiming victory in a war that was just starting. "We got those bastards! Who's next?"

Right in the midst of this, I went with my family to a local park. My kids were toddlers at the time, and the park was our friend because it provided wide open space where energy could be exerted without things getting broken. On this particular day the park was quiet with only one other family present. This family's children were playing soccer. When one kid has a ball and the other does not, the one without is going to quickly make friends with the one who has. This is exactly what happened, and all the kids were soon playing and laughing together. They didn't have a care in the world, and they certainly were not concerned by the difference in their shades of skin tone.

The courteous thing to do in this situation is to walk over and make small-talk with the other parents, which is exactly what we did. Based on what the couple was wearing, it was apparent that they were Muslim. According to the aforementioned faith leaders in our country, it should have been logical for me to assume that for this couple and this family to live out their faith, they should, in that moment, have been considering how to harm us in the name of Allah. So what does one do with a family who has a mission of killing us? Invite them over for dinner, obviously!

We were having such a nice time chatting and found out that we lived in the same general neck of the woods, so we excitedly invited them over for a meal the following week. They were from Saudi Arabia, and they brought over some food unique to their culture. We made some of our favorite dishes, and we all had a wonderful time together. They shared about their life and faith and at one point stopped in the middle of a conversation to pray. We didn't try to convert one another. Instead, our entire time was focused on beliefs we had in common. We talked about Jesus, God, Allah, and Moham-mad and genuinely desired to learn and grow from our time together. And here is the crazy thing: they never once tried to kill us. We came away from our time together without a scratch. Who would have thought?

One of the easiest ways to get a lot of people interested in what you are doing is to create common enemies. The church has become masterful at this throughout history. Once a common enemy is iden-tified, the subtle work of dehumanization can commence. When I was introduced to the evangelical church, common enemies were abundant and obvious. Anyone of a different faith was an enemy, and to my surprise this included all those Catholics I grew up with. People who were not straight were most certainly common enemies since there is obviously nothing God hates quite as much as gay peo-ple. Democrats were a common enemy, and I could go on and on. I once saw a quote that said, "There is no hate like good Christian love." As soon as these enemies were publicly and relentlessly identi-fied, they were treated as the other. When a group of people is treated like the other, the dehumanizing process is under way. Simply refer to any genocide ever in the history of the world, and you can see how this works. Or if that feels too distant, look to the history of racism in the United States. When you see the pictures of Black men, women, and children hanging from trees, let your eyes look down and notice the clergy members who are often standing under their feet.

One of the most common comments I get based on the work I engage in is something along the lines of, "I'm not like you. I don't feel the need to question everything. I just believe with blind faith." When I hear this, I am reminded of a story from Germany during

World War II. There was a church just a short distance from a rail-road that was regularly used to carry humans to a concentration camp. One warm Sunday morning congregants were meeting for church when the sound of a train approaching was heard. The pastor stood up, closed all the windows, and motioned for the organist to begin playing and leading a hymn. As human beings were being car-ried to a death camp, the church averted their eyes, plugged their ears, and sang to Jesus. That, my friends, is that danger of "blind faith." Blind faith consistently ignores the cries of the oppressed.

In the same vein, people often scoff at me when I get on my soapbox about refusing to attend a church that is not fully affirming of everyone, including people who are not straight and people who are not men. I will often get responses that make it seem as if I am going over the top with my actions and views. My response remains consistent. "If your church did not allow people of color to get mar-ried there, would you still attend?" So what is the difference? To me, this nightmare that has reared its ugly head consistently over the past several decades is not just a theological issue; it is a civil rights issue. And until we stop closing our church windows and singing louder, we will continue to hurt, oppress, and ignore.

At my Catholic school on the wall between two of the classrooms was a larger-than-life picture of Jesus. This picture portrayed him with long, flowing sandy-blond hair, Caucasian skin, and a beautiful white robe. I never once questioned why Jesus looked so much like me even though in those very classrooms we were learning about the differences between various cultures. That was not at all a picture of Jesus. That was some made-up superhero who was created within the belief structure that to be white and American is to be right and free. The truth is that Jesus actually looked very little like me and an awful lot like my Muslim friend who came over with his family to share a meal all those years later. And not only did he physically look more like him, he also acted a lot more like him. This man and his family accepted me, my wife, and my children in spite of our faith differences and in spite of the difference of our skin color. We laughed, we ate, we talked, and we embraced. It was true, it was authentic, it was lovely, and it was real.

The Jesus we claim to follow was intentionally and overtly focused on diversity and inclusion. The story of the good Samaritan, the story of the woman at the well, the fact that he chose such a unique group of disciples—he didn't care if a person was religious or if they were filled with demons. He didn't care if they were male, female, or other. He didn't care if they were adults or children. He didn't care if they were rich or poor. Jesus was for everyone. Why aren't we?

Bring It Home

The best part about visiting my parents is that when I walk in the door, I feel welcomed. I come in, throw my luggage on the guest bed, go to the fridge, grab a beer, and sit down at the table. I never wonder if any of that is okay because I know it is. On top of that, my parents often will have some special cookies or candy out and a nice dinner planned because they knew I was coming. So not only am I welcomed, I am even treated with preference. Dad often gets his two cents in about how mom never makes cookies for him. But wait—it gets even better. Not only am I welcomed, my wife and my kids are welcomed in the same way. (Other than the fact that the kids are not allowed to have the beer and Suzie prefers wine.)

Our spiritual journey home should be welcoming to everyone around us. Our spiritual home should feel safe to all, not just a select few. For this news about Jesus to be good for anyone, it has to be good for everyone. The Bible says that "Jesus died once and for all" (Romans 6:10). The fancy Greek word for *all* still just means *all*.

On your journey, be sure that all are welcome. And when you sense in your heart that someone is not, ask the hard questions about why. Find the root of it and tear it all the way out so it is unable to return.

One of the most interesting and repeated questions that comes up when I bring up my thoughts on everyone having a place in heaven is, "What about Hitler?" Thankfully, I am not the one to answer this question for all, but I say yes and amen to Hitler as well as to all other humans who failed terribly at their humanity. *All* means all.

11

Inconsistency

There is nothing constant in this world but inconsistency.

—Jonathan Swift

DURING THE EARLY DAYS OF my conservative evangelical experience, I was the drummer for a Christian band, and many of the events we played for were geared toward teenagers. At one point I was in the youth room in the basement of a church where we were performing, and when I looked to my right, I noticed a mural covering the entire wall. The painting was of a group of teenagers in a boat pulling other teenagers out of flames—and the name of the youth group was Rescue. The painting was shocking, first because I had no idea why there was a boat floating above a fiery pit, and second because it showed kids in danger of burning alive. This was the moment I started asking the question, *Is this really what I believe? Do I really believe that the God of the universe desires us to believe in him the correct way, or else the obvious consequence is an eternity burning in hell?*

Years later when I had ascended to the ranks of a church staff member, I was informed that I was supposed to attend a special event. First I was told it was a drama, to which I thought, *Oh, crap.* I grew up loving Broadway musicals, and the atrocity of the modern

Christian drama is something the artist world should never be expected to forgive! Then I was told that the name of it was "Heaven's Gates, Hell's Flames," and I upgraded my thought to, *Oh, shit!* I was thinking of that painting from the youth room and was naturally assuming that something like that was going to be portrayed in the form of an unfortunate Christian drama. And the even better news was, as the director of music and arts at the church, I got the blessing of paying for this out of my own budget!

The big day arrived, and I came in and took my place in the back of the sanctuary. I don't mean the back seat—I mean as far back as I could be while still actually being in the room. I stood against the back wall as the drama unfolded. I watched in horror as members of the church participated as actors in this twisted narrative. There was the drunk and drugged-out teenage character, the loose woman character, and the atheist dad character. Of course, there was the devil character with all his demons and the star of the show, Jesus, who was one of the church board members. The characters who couldn't get their shit together had an opportunity to grab on to Jesus' hand to be led into eternal bliss, represented by a white door with bright lights shining from behind. But unfortunately, several chose their vices over Jesus and were quite literally dragged by the demon characters kicking and screaming through a door into fake flames that were illuminated by red flashing lights and blown around furiously by strategically placed fans. The ending involved someone turning away from their sins, accepting Jesus, and changing their ways. This was followed by the leader of the drama group coming to the front of the stage to explain to all of us poor souls about the choice that we all have. We can choose heaven or we can choose hell. It's just that simple. He asked people to raise their hands if they wanted to be certain they would get to go to heaven and did a heartfelt, slow, repeat-after-me prayer followed by rousing applause from the rest of the heaven-goers in the room.

This, my friends, is the definition of fucked up. The following year they told me that the group was being welcomed back. I informed them that my budget wasn't paying for it and that I wasn't showing up or telling anyone about it. They still did it, I didn't pay for it, and I most certainly did not show up.

Every week at church we are told about this *agape* love which is supposed to mean an intense, almost romantic type of love that God has for us. And in the same church service where this love is preached, we are also informed that this all-loving and all-knowing God is completely fine with sending us to be tortured for all eternity if we don't believe the right things in the right ways. And all together we are informed that this is called grace. I do not call this grace at all. I call this bullshit at the highest level (if there are levels of bullshit, that is).

Everywhere else in our culture, when "love" is based on fear, we call it abuse. We tell the victim to get the hell out of that relationship and oftentimes call the authorities. The *love-me-like-I-tell-you-to-or-you-will-get-hurt* relationship is everyone's worst nightmare, unless you are an evangelical Christian, in which case it is considered the most complete and truest version of love a person could ever experience. Everywhere else in our culture when "grace" is based on doing things the "right" way, it is called manipulation. True grace is when someone doesn't do things your way and you still accept them.

I was tempted to call this book *This All Sounds Crazy When You Say It Out Loud* but was advised against it. But honestly, when we take away the religious facade and just listen to what is being said at face value, it is batshit crazy. Yet millions of people continue to raise their hands and walk blindly forward. Why? Because they are scared out of their minds not to, and because being a part of the in-crowd feels good. Being certain is a feeling of freedom. Unfortunately, that certainty is built on a desire for gain and a desire for dominance, historically speaking. Growth occurs and finances flow when people feel like they are a part of the "truth." And that "truth" must be protected at all costs.

All right—time to take a step down from the soapbox and get back to reality here. When I share my sentiments about hell and salvation with people, most of the time they agree. But the problem comes when trying to think about what faith without certainty looks like. I am not advocating for a faith without certainty. Instead, I am simply rethinking what certainty means. I will often get questions such as, "So you don't believe hell is real?" or "Are you a universalist?" or "Then what is the point of Jesus?" Question one, no I don't believe in hell like the modern church has taught. Question two, that all depends on what your view of a universalist is. If it is that everyone gets to go to heaven, then absolutely. Question three, the point of Jesus is so many things—and if Jesus' only importance was his death and resurrection, we are missing out on so much.

Just humor me here for a few moments. Even if you do not want to go along with the "hell is not real" idea I am proposing, think about what faith and life in general would be like if we at least lived as if hell were not real. Our goal would go from appealing to fear to focusing on love. What would our churches and our world look like if the focus were not on scaring people into heaven but simply on helping others to fall in love with the life and work of Jesus and with each other? Imagine the energy and time we would have to fight injustice and stand up for the oppressed if we didn't have to worry about saving everyone from the flames of hell. So many relationships would be restored, and so much abuse would be avoided. It wouldn't be good for the bottom line, and church attendance would likely decline, but the flip side is that the world would be a better and more beautiful place.

A little while back I was asked to lead a Bible study for a group of people from a local church I spoke at. First of all, let's state the obvious: questionable decision-making on their part. This group was primarily made up of older people, and the only reason I point that out is because their generation includes food at most church functions. During our Bible study we had an actual intermission where we all got up from the table and enjoyed the potluck meal everyone pitched in to provide. After my second deviled egg, I looked over and noticed a middle-aged man standing by himself in the corner with tear-filled eyes. I put down my plate of food and walked over to see what was going on. He proceeded to tell me how a number of years ago his wife died from cancer. When she passed, their son was a teenager. After watching his mom suffer and eventually die, this young man got very angry at God for taking his mom. He disassociated from God, church, and anything to do with religion, because who would want to follow a horrible god that would take away a kid's mom? Who could blame him? Fast-forward several years and this kid graduates from high school and decides to join the military. And that week this man found out that his son was being deployed to a combat situation in the Middle East. Maybe you are starting to follow where this is going. The father was in tears because his son no longer believed in God and was now going to a combat zone. He was worried that his son would get killed and be rewarded for his bravery by spending eternity being tortured in hell. I did not feel this to be the appropriate time to share my dispensation on hell not being real. So instead, I put my hand on his shoulder, looked him in the eye and said, "I think that the grace of God is far greater than we can ever imagine, and I believe that this all-loving God fully understands your son's pain." He looked up at me, and I quite literally saw his shoulders lower as he hugged me and said thank you. The following week he came up to me and shared how freeing and healing my comments were for him.

It's simple, really. Maybe God's love is far greater than our feeble theologies. Love in its purest form does not allow people to be tortured for all eternity. If that is indeed true, we are wrong on one of two things. Either God is not all that loving, or hell the way it has been taught is not true. Life will be better lived believing in an actual all-loving God. Because if love equals torture, I am out altogether!

Bring It Home

It is likely that part of the reason you are trying to find your faith again is because portions of the religion you followed feel inconsistent with the God you desire. Be free to believe differently. Don't be afraid to get rid of what you were taught in order to grab onto something better.

When I started questioning many core theologies of the modern church, I was surprised when my research revealed I was not alone. I was amazed that the things taught to me as absolute truths were not always the acceptable belief systems within Christianity. And at the end of the day, it's more about *how* we believe than *what* we believe. If I am wrong about hell and people feel more valued, loved, and cared for because of it, I am okay with that.

Coming up with better answers or better theology should never be the goal. The goal should instead be to care for others no matter what. And if our theology rubs against that, it may be wise to rethink some things.

12

Rethinking Greatness

Each of us has some basic goodness which is the foundation
for the greatness we can ultimately achieve.

—Les Brown

I LIVE IN A MEDIUM-SIZED community where pretty much every church is one of two types. One type consists of dying mainline churches with large buildings that are maybe half full on a good Sunday. We are now at the place in history much like what was seen in Europe not too long ago where old church buildings are being sold to be made into other things or are being taken over by young, hip new churches who believe the old architecture will attract people to their vintage vibe. The other type of church is your typical modern evangelical church, often in a boxy building, with the rock music, coffee, and a relaxed-looking pastor who gives out the spiritual pep talk of the week.

I felt that maybe it was time to attack the status quo in our community and try something different. I had this idea that only seemed to make sense to me. Every time I would share it with someone, I would receive a variety of different reasons why it wouldn't work. My rationale was this: if Jesus focused most of his energy on the sick, the broken, the outcasts, the sinners, and the poor, why not start a community for exactly those people? Screw the fancy building and the slick sermons; let's just create a place for the type of people who hung around Jesus.

We started in the way a typical church plant would: my wife Suzie and I went to a church-planting assessment to judge whether or not we had what it took. I confused the hell out of them because nothing I wanted to do fit with their ideal mold. I am confident I simply wore down the man who was insisting I have a clear plan to "get people across the line of salvation." I informed him that I wasn't confident where the line was and therefore was unsure how to encourage people to cross it. As with so many times in my life, I skirted through with talent and wit, and for some reason unknown to me, I was told that I received their blessing to start a church. I don't think that is what I came looking for, but it did feel nice, and we met some lovely people along the way. Suzie and I wasted no time. On the way home we were on the phone calling people and inviting them to our house. For several months we had twenty to thirty people meeting in our unfinished basement, talking about starting a church. After a while this started feeling monotonous and boring, so I let them know about the plan to start a church for the hurting and homeless, which resulted in fewer people showing up each week. When we finally moved out of the basement and into our new space, only two people from the original thirty stuck with us. Apparently this church-for-the-people-Jesus-hung-out-with idea didn't have a lot of mass appeal.

We were confident that the community would need to be downtown because that was where most of the outcasts in our city hung out. A pastor friend of mine mentioned that there was a business with a garage attached to it downtown and that the owner of the business attended his church. We went with him to take a look at the space, and let me tell you, it looked like an absolute piece of shit. Suzie and I immediately knew this was our new church building. One thing they do not teach you at the church-planting assessment is how to approach a business owner to ask them if you can start a church for poor and homeless people in their garage. I figured the best idea was to find a way to meet the owner face-to-face, so I simply went to the church I knew she attended the following Sunday. I had spoken at this church a few times and wasn't a complete stranger. Suzie had led music there a handful of times as well. I knew the business owner's name from my pastor friend, and it wasn't that big of a church, so I figured I could find her and invite her to lunch or coffee.

I asked around, and after being pointed in her direction, I approached her with a smile. Her name was Judy, she stood no more than five feet tall, and she was at least in her late sixties. I held out my hand to her and introduced myself. She looked up into my eyes with an intense yet kind conviction and said, "I know who you are. You are Matt, and last time you were here speaking, I looked at you and knew that you and your wife are supposed to start a ministry in my building." At the same time we were praying about starting a ministry downtown, Judy was praying for someone to start a ministry downtown in her building. And so we did.

We began our new church with a meal and a worship service, just to see if anyone would be interested in hanging out with us. A group of us came early in the week to clean up the garage and move out junk, sweep, and set up chairs. We hung fabric on the walls and did everything to make the garage into something beautiful—and by beautiful, I mean a place that was at least safe and warm with as much of the bare walls covered as possible. The big day came. The band set up, the sound system was put in place, food was brought in, and tables were set. That evening the place filled to capacity with all sorts of people from every background imaginable. At the time, it was quite possibly the most diverse gathering our little city had ever seen.

No one, including myself, really knew what this was, so I thought most of the people who came were simply curious. I welcomed everyone, the band was spectacular, the message was full of inspiration and emotion, and the food was fabulous. I let them know that we would plan to be back every week with more of the same. After most people left, a pastor friend of mine approached me. I naturally assumed he was going to shower me with accolades for the great work I did to pull this off. I assumed he was going to ask where all the people came from and say that this was the type of work needed to make a difference in our city. Instead, he approached me with a solemn look on his face, looked me in the eyes with all sincerity, and said something I will never forget. He said, "You drove into this neighborhood with a Cadillac when everyone else is driving around in rusty old Pintos." To be fair, I actually arrived in a rusty 1995 red Ford F-150, but his sentiment was loud and clear. Greatness is not what hurting people want or need. Immediately my mind went to a Bible verse out of the Old Testament that I was made aware of by the great activist and author John Perkins. It says,

> I hate, I despise your feasts,
>   and I take no delight in your solemn assemblies.
> Even though you offer me your burnt offerings and grain offerings,
>   I will not accept them;
> and the peace offerings of your fattened animals,
>   I will not look upon them.

Take away from me the noise of your songs;
   to the melody of your harps I will not listen.
But let justice roll down like waters,
   and righteousness like an ever-flowing stream.

(Amos 5:21–24 ESV)

My life of trying to be the absolute best at everything led me to assume that everyone is like me and that they value greatness above all else. Great music only matters so much to the person who fights every moment of every day with years of trauma and deep wounds of abandonment. Fancy food only matters so much to the person struggling with mental health to the point that they are unable to function. An inspirational message only matters so much to a person who has been without hope for decades. Nice table settings and decor only matter so much to the person about to venture outside to find a place to sleep for the night. Instead of asking what the people who would attend wanted, I naively assumed that everyone wanted what I wanted without considering the reality that we are not only looking through different lenses; we are living in different worlds.

We certainly live in a culture where greatness is rewarded. And rightfully so! Greatness requires an immense amount of time, energy, and research, and when it is achieved, it is often a wonderful benefit to the world. Great authors, artists, musicians, educators, tradespeople, and medical professionals make this world a better place to be in. Watching someone who is great at their craft is an incredible experience. Seeing them effortlessly accomplish what to most would seem unthinkable is nothing short of remarkable.

I have spent a good portion of my life pursuing passion, and I still do to this day. When I was in middle school all the way through college, I practiced the drums for an average of two to three hours every day. I had no interest in getting beat out for any auditions, and the commitment paid off time and time again. When I became a public speaker, I pored over videos of other speakers, analyzing everything they did. I had people give me critiques and would listen to recordings in order to fix and adjust nuances. I'd learn my script or outline so well I could spend the entire time focusing on the details, watching faces to identify what was working and what was falling flat. I am pro-greatness through and through.

But when we are experiencing emotional hurt, feelings of not being enough, or feelings of being alone and abandoned, greatness is not what is needed. Goodness is what truly heals the heart and soul. I have spent my entire career working on justice issues in our world, and I have had the amazing opportunity to meet with countless people who are sacrificially and tirelessly working to make the lives of others better—to create a more humane world. And although many of these wonderful people are great at what they do, what matters most is their goodness. That goodness is what defines their humanity and their actions.

During moments in life when hurt has seemed overwhelming, I have always hated when people recommend a "great" book or a "great" podcast. Sure, these things can be helpful, but in the midst of hurt and pain, what I desire is goodness. I want someone to ask how I am doing. I want someone to look me in the eye and simply care. I want people to knock on my door even if I told them not to. In the midst of intense pain, greatness falls short. In the midst of injustice, greatness is lacking.

The entire week after our spectacular garage event full of all sorts of greatness, my friend's words continued to echo in my mind:

You drove into this neighborhood with a Cadillac when everyone else is driving around in rusty old Pintos. He was right. I wanted greatness when all those who came were needing, looking for, and desiring goodness. The next weekend we took down the decor, got rid of the sound system, set up tables, and ordered pizza. No agenda, no great music or message of hope. Just tables of people talking and eating across from and beside each other. Listening, laughing, hurting, and healing in the absence of greatness. Goodness took over, and for the next eight years, people felt loved, cared for, and heard. We became great at goodness.

For those eight years the goal became simple. Everyone who came in the door was going to experience love, and everyone who came in the door was going to be invited to be a part of the community. That little garage was transformed into a pretty cool space over the years, with new bathrooms, a full kitchen, fresh paint, and a pretty sweet glass garage door. We housed a food pantry, held epic neighborhood block parties, and even opened an employment program and a transitional housing program. What started as a crazy idea that no one thought would work turned into something special and memorable. And best of all, it was meaningful because greatness took a backseat to goodness.

Bring It Home

In the midst of discovering yourself and desiring to help others, focus more on your goodness than on your greatness. From personal experience I can confidently say that when people love you because of your greatness, you often end up alone. Think of the people you enjoy spending time with. Do you enjoy being with them because of what they are great at, or do you enjoy spending time with them because they are good people?

Don't ever give up on the pursuit of greatness; we need more great ideas and more great skilled people to do the hard work that's in front of us. But never sacrifice your goodness in pursuit of it.

13

Expectations

I'm not in this world to live up to your expectations and
you're not in this world to live up to mine.

—Bruce Lee

FOR ANYONE WHO HAS NOT worked hands-on with struggling populations, I can assure you that it is not for the faint of heart, and it sounds much more appealing and exciting than it actually is. In reality it is brutally difficult, and it breaks your heart over and over again. The moment you think there is a breakthrough, you turn around to discover that the cycle of poverty is an absolute vortex that almost never lets go.

I'll never forget the feeling of excitement when we accepted our first transitional housing tenant, a single mother and her teenage daughter who were literally living in a tent. I'll also never forget the sadness and brokenness I felt six months later when I had to evict them because they absolutely trashed the place. I will never forget the hope we had for a young couple trying to make it work amid suffocating circumstances who eventually ended up getting an apartment of their own. I'll also never forget the shock and disbelief of walking into that apartment when they were in the middle of a meth binge. Unfortunately I could go on with these stories. Our goal quickly went from helping people out of poverty to helping people into community, and that was certainly more possible and more fulfilling.

Something happened in the early days of our little community of misfits that should have given me insight into what was coming. I was a prison chaplain at the same time I was leading what we named B-Side Community, which gave me a lot of street cred with our congregation. It gave me a relational foot in the door because many who came had been in prison or had friends or family members in jail. Working at the prison made me more approachable because of my firsthand understanding of what life in prison was like. Many felt as if I could relate to them, and they also felt that I wouldn't judge them. They were correct.

One young man, Danny, was originally introduced to me by his substance abuse counselor. He wasn't a regular part of our community but would come and go and stop by a lot throughout the week to talk with me when he knew I was around. Although Danny had many demons in his closet, the biggest challenge he faced from day to day was a feeling of abandonment that began from his experience growing up with a mother who was rarely present. This was something we talked about at great lengths, and I personally felt that he was making some impressive strides forward. After I'd known him several months, he came to me with an opportunity that I hoped would be a breakthrough for him.

A relative of his from out of state had recently passed away, and his mother, the one who was at the root of his abandonment issues, was offering to drive him to Tennessee for the funeral. He received approval from his parole agent to be out of state for two days and was expected at the agent's desk immediately upon his return. My optimistic mind went straight to thoughts of mother-and-son bonding time in the car and forgiveness during the shared experience of grieving the loss of a loved one. Although this did happen to some degree, their time together ended with an explosive argument and culminated with Danny's mother driving away, back to Wisconsin, leaving him alone and abandoned again. Instead of forgiveness, another level of bitterness was built. Instead of restoration, another depth of hatred was discovered. And to top it off, if Danny didn't find a way home quickly, he would be heading back to prison for violating his parole. That is the moment my phone rang.

Danny was on the other end of the line in tears, and my heart was broken for the first of what would end up being a million times at B-Side. I knew I couldn't leave him down there, and I went straight to work finding a solution. I hopped online and found an option to get Danny home in time on a Greyhound bus. I called our two other board members and shared with them the story. Together we agreed that even though our little organization was not in the financial or organizational place to be giving handouts, it was more important that we did what we felt to be the right thing. We had no way of verifying Danny's story but did not want to add to his abandonment trauma. I wanted to be the person who said, "I see you, I believe you, and I am here for you." I quickly purchased the ticket, phoned Danny with the information, and simply asked him to come see me as soon as he had a chance. Although I heard he made it back safely, I did not see him the following week, or the week after that, and he didn't return any of my calls. After several weeks of concern, confusion, and disappointment, I finally found Danny.

Following a regular Sunday-evening meal and gathering, my wife and I locked up the building and headed home, exhausted as usual from an evening of caring for, listening to, and serving those in our community. We got home, put our young children to bed, and collapsed into our own bed to watch a little television to decompress. It was 10:00 p.m., we couldn't afford cable, and Netflix wasn't a thing yet, so one of our very few options was the local news. I remember chatting with Suzie and then looking up at the news broadcast only to see a picture of Danny staring back at me. I quickly turned up the volume to hear the story of how he had robbed thirteen houses over the past three weeks before being apprehended by authorities. I turned off the TV, looked over at Suzie, and said, "I bought him a bus ticket back home, and he thanked me by breaking into thirteen houses. If I would have just left his ass there, this wouldn't have happened."

I could never begin to explain the feelings I was having in that moment. I was pissed off beyond belief, I was sad, and I was confused. I felt betrayed, I felt guilty, I felt responsible, and I felt like a fool. And of course, because I was so proud of helping Danny, I had shared the story of helping him with several people, leaving me feeling utterly embarrassed.

After a couple weeks passed, I received a phone call from the local jail chaplain to let me know that there was an inmate there who was requesting to see me. This was not unusual since visits to the jail were a necessary part of our community. I asked who it was, and, of course, it was Danny. I did not immediately give the chaplain an answer because I was not sure I could face him. What would I possibly say to him? How could I possibly see him without saying things I would later regret? After soliciting advice from people I trusted, I decided to go, not to say anything but simply to listen.

I gave the security guard my ID, walked through the thick metal doors of the jail, and sat down on the cold metal stool facing the plexiglass that would separate us during our conversation. Danny walked in with his head hanging low and tears in his eyes. He picked up the telephone that was used to communicate. I followed suit and picked up the other line. He didn't speak, and it was several minutes before Danny mustered the courage to look at me. At first it was a quick glance, and then after another couple of moments he looked me in the eyes, and a few tears trickled down his face. I didn't say a word. I just waited for him to begin the conversation.

Danny began with an apology. It seemed heartfelt, although an incarcerated man tends to begin his journey with a good dose of emotion. He shared how he made it home and shortly thereafter ran into his former drug dealer. He relapsed and went downhill fast. Danny did not have a job or any money and therefore began stealing in order to pay for his reawakened addiction. He thanked me for my kindness and told me that he was far too ashamed of himself to come find me. He said he felt like a failure and he felt like he let me down. He was certainly correct about the second part.

Then Danny said something I did not see coming. He said that he felt so guilty for letting me down and for stealing from innocent people that he wanted to somehow make things right. Without any prompting from the authorities and without any promise of leniency in sentencing, Danny risked his own safety by giving up the name of his drug dealer, as well as incriminating evidence against him. This happened to be one of the biggest dealers in our city. The man was apprehended within a matter of days and was taken off the streets of our little city. On his way down, as an attempt at amends, Danny decided to do what he could to make the neighborhood he vandalized and stole from a safer place.

Danny broke my heart, and he also stole from me. He stole some of my ability to trust. He stole some of my ability to believe in the best in others. He stole a bit of my ability to believe that love always wins. He even stole some of my ability to believe that God is good, since my relationship with God was most certainly the catalyst for my relationship with Danny. But Danny also gave me so much. He gave me a hard introduction to the reality and challenge of addiction. He gave me an awakening to the fact that kindness and compassion are not foolproof ways to fix deep-rooted problems of abuse and abandonment. All the kindness and love in the world is not capable of fixing all the brokenness.

The one thing Danny did not steal from me was my desire to keep trying. Even though he was simply the first of many letdowns, to this day I choose to default to compassion, kindness, and love. Although I no longer expect these actions to universally change realities, I do know that they can. And even if my actions don't change others, they will change me. Every loving word that exits my lips changes me into a better human being. Every act of compassion that comes from my hands changes me to become more like the Jesus I desire to emulate. Every look of compassion that comes from my eyes softens my old, calloused heart. This has had a perfect track record. My attempts to love and care change me every time and change others every once in a while. I had no control over Danny's response. The only control I had was the ability to choose to stop everything, pick up the phone, and purchase a bus ticket. My prayer is that no amount of disappointment, hurt, or embarrassment will ever keep me from trying.

Bring It Home

Maybe it's because of commercials or movies, but we have certainly adopted a false sense of reality when it comes to helping others, especially when it comes to helping others in difficult situations. It is good and possibly even necessary for our journey of faith to be linked intimately with justice. And when I say "justice," I mean lifting up the oppressed as opposed to convicting those in the wrong. The Old Testament of the Bible alludes to God and justice meeting together on earth as a kiss (Psalm 85:10). John Mark McMillan's song "He Loves Us" was neutered by the contemporary Christian music industry when his lyrics "Heaven meets earth like a sloppy wet kiss" were replaced with "unforeseen kiss." If you want to play it safe while kissing, a closed-mouth peck is the way to go. It is really difficult to mess that up. But a closed-mouth peck is not all that different from a fist bump and will bring little to no excitement. A deep, passionate, emotion-filled, open-mouthed kiss, on the other hand, is all kinds of exciting. But it is almost always less than perfect. Teeth hit together, one person turns one way while the other goes another way. All sorts of crazy stuff can happen, and it is all well worth it. The reality is that justice is an open-mouthed kiss, and it is sloppy and messy as hell.

As you humbly try to connect with the divine, you are almost certain to be drawn to those who are hurting. When you are, simply remove any desired results from your head and be in the moment that has been afforded you. Be a blessing without needing a perfect result.

Sometimes it's the simple things that make the biggest difference, like when my friend put her hand on the shoulder of a homeless man and asked him how he was doing. He responded by asking her why she touched him. He said, "No one ever touches me." Sometimes the greatness is in the attention and not in the healing. Maybe the power of Jesus was less in his healing of the sick and more in the touching and giving attention to the broken.

Most people who are homeless stay homeless no matter how many meals we volunteer to serve them. Many women who are rescued from the sex trade go back to it. Hundreds of wells dug in developing countries eventually break down. According to the National Institute of Justice seventy-five percent of the inmates released from prison end up going back within five years.[1] As we walk back home, simply be willing to love those you meet along the way without any expectations of how they should receive that love.

1. https://worldpopulationreview.com/state-rankings/recidivism-rates-by-state.

14

Success

Don't aim for success if you want it; just do what you love
and believe in, and it will come naturally.

—David Frost

BECAUSE I AM A MUSIC lover, I came up with the name B-Side for our
little church community. Back in the days when everyone bought
records, specifically singles, the song everyone wanted to hear was
on the A-side. On the B-side was the song no one knew. It was a song
the artist hoped the listener would give a chance to. We were the
ragtag group that just wanted to be given a chance. While the rest of
the world went to church in nice buildings on the outskirts of town,
we hung out in our little refurbished garage in the poorest neighborhood of our city. Another interesting point about our location is that
just across the street was the part of the city in which all sorts of
development was happening, with new apartments, business buildings, and a performing arts center. If you want to see an A-side and a
B-side, just stand in the middle of Madison Street. On one side is
prosperity and money, and on the other, not so much.

One beautiful day early in our existence, we were having our
Sunday evening gathering with the garage door open, hoping to get
a little bit of that 1950s nostalgic feel, when a man pulled up with a

flat tire. He stopped in because he saw the door open and assumed we were a car-repair business. He walked in looking for help with his flat, and not only did we help with the tire, we also invited him to stay for a meal we had prepared. He took us up on the offer and kept coming back for nearly seven years.

Dennis was a man who had a very difficult life. He grew up on the streets of Chicago in poverty and joined a violent gang as a teenager. As with most gang members, he ended up in prison for several years and upon his release hopped on a bus to get away from all the negative influences of his childhood home. He landed in our city and because of a flat tire became one of the most endearing people in our little community.

During the time Dennis was a part of B-Side, we helped him find a job, gave him a place to live, and got him involved on the leadership team. Who better to help lead a group of people struggling with poverty and addiction than a person who has struggled with poverty and addiction? Dennis had a vibrant personality, and when he was in front of a crowd he seemed at home. I asked him to speak a handful of Sundays, and eventually he started a Sunday morning breakfast program that became extremely popular. Dennis had an infectious spirit and a willingness to talk with anyone anywhere, which led him to become the shining example of what it looks like to climb out of darkness and succeed. He was being invited to speak at churches and other nonprofits and was starting to amass quite a reputation throughout the city. One lesson I learned over years of working with people who have challenging backgrounds is that leadership and attention has the potential to go really bad, really fast. This was certainly the case with Dennis.

He grabbed onto the power and influence he was given with both hands and was not interested in letting it go. Dennis began demanding more and more and became an expert at manipulation in order to get whatever it was he desired. If he couldn't get it from me, he would simply move on to the next person who was available and willing. Eventually, the people he desired to serve, along with many who were committed to supporting him, began to see that something was off. Within a year he went from the guy everyone loved and wanted to be around to the reason people were no longer coming to B-Side and the reason people and churches were pulling funding and volunteers.

One of my greatest strengths and weaknesses is that I do not easily give up on people. When everyone else wanted to give up on Dennis, I was committing to meet with him more and was trying desperately to get the train back on the rails. Nothing was working, and things simply kept getting worse. This all reached a crescendo when I received a call from one of our leadership team members who also employed Dennis and provided him a place to rent.

I picked up the phone and was informed that Dennis had been badly burned in an apartment fire. I didn't ask any questions but simply hung up the phone and headed over to Saint Paul, Minnesota, to visit him in the burn unit. He was in rough shape. It turned out that he had relapsed and locked himself in his bathroom. Intentionally or unintentionally a fire was started, and Dennis had to be rescued. It became obvious to me in that moment that I was going to need to have a really hard conversation with him after he recovered. Everything was going downhill for him so fast, and all the hard work and dedication he'd put in now seemed to be spiraling backward.

After being released from the hospital, Dennis returned to B-Side fully expecting to continue leading, speaking, and organizing. But at this point he had not only burned himself, he had burned virtually every relational bridge he had. I was going to have to be the bearer of some bad news that I knew would not go over well. I set up a meeting with Dennis and a couple of other guys who knew him well for accountability and safety. I looked him in the eyes and shared with him my concerns as well as my hopes and told him that he would no longer be allowed to have any leadership roles for the time being. He looked me straight in the eyes, told me I was the Antichrist, stood up, and stormed out of the room.

I spent hundreds of hours with Dennis. B-Side had invested thousands of dollars in him. And when it was all said and done, I felt as if I failed him miserably to the point that he left in a worse place than when he came. And over the years he wasn't the only one. People would come, we would help them get on their feet, they would get involved, serve, lead, and ultimately leave angry. Dennis called me the Antichrist, Mark warned me to watch my back, Sue said I used her, Pops told me to go fuck myself. After a while I had to start asking the question, *Why is there a pattern that always ends up with me being the bad guy and them leaving?*

After years of thinking about this and losing sleep over it, I finally found what felt like clarity. I had a definition of what I thought success was. Success for someone like Dennis, in my mind, was getting a job, having a place to live, and ultimately becoming a leader. This is the American dream. And when people from difficult backgrounds accomplish any of this, we tend to parade them around as the true success stories of our world. But what if that isn't actually success? Maybe a person could be unemployed and still a success. Maybe a person could be homeless and still a success. Is it possible for success to be less about what we do and accomplish and more about simply who we are?

After Dennis left, I gathered our leadership team together and drew a circle on a whiteboard. I told them that no longer would our success be defined by how many homeless people got off the streets or by how many people got jobs or how many stayed out of jail. If that was success, we were the hub of failure. At the top of the circle I wrote, "Everyone is loved," on one side of the circle I wrote, "Everyone belongs," and on the other side I wrote, "We are honest and authentic." If you came through our garage door, you were going to be loved and valued. If you came through our garage door, you were going to be invited to be a part of a community that cared. And if you came through the garage door, we were going to be honest with you. I told the team that if we did those three things over and over, we would be a success.

In the same way that people didn't get excited about or understand my vision of creating a church for outcasts, our leadership team was not overly optimistic about my new definition of success. It turned out that my new success model didn't fit with the thoughts of a team that was much more interested in proper discipleship, salvation of souls, and the gospel being preached as often as possible. It turned out my success model did not fit well with the churches funding us, who wanted stories of people getting off the streets and becoming contributing members of society. Within two years I locked the doors of the B-Side garage for the last time.

I walked across the street and turned around at the same corner where I had stood with my pastor friend and my wife eight years prior. What once was a huge eyesore was now, well, a little less of an eyesore. New paint and a new garage door, functioning bathrooms and a commercial kitchen. So much time and effort. So much hope. So much belief. And it was now over because love wasn't enough to keep the doors open. As I turned away from B-Side to walk away for the last time, I felt two things. The first was a desire to punch a wall. I had never been so angry in my entire life. The second was the ability to take a deep breath for the first time since that first meal.

In the middle of writing this book, I ran into Dennis at the grocery store. He greeted Suzie and me with the same infectious smile I remembered from years ago, but something seemed off. A little while later Dennis showed up in the news. He was arrested for stabbing a man outside a local bar. A few months after that, I received a phone call from an old friend who informed me that Dennis had relapsed, overdosed, and died. May his tortured soul now rest in peace. I feel honored and blessed to have had the opportunity to attempt to love and care for Dennis while he was here. And I trust that God forgives me for the ways I let him down.

Bring It Home

As we journey back home, it is important to remember that the opinions of others and the results of our attempts don't determine our success. If people think you are crazy for leaving church or for believing differently, you are in good company. You are in the company of pretty much every important character in the Bible, including the greatest heretic of them all, Jesus. If you feel shattered and alone apart from your previous church community, you can join me and everyone else who has walked away with a limp and felt the deep pain of loss.

In a perfect world, we do the right thing and it feels good. Everything gets buttoned up with a good ending that involves hugs and high fives. Unfortunately that perfect world we all long for rarely, if ever, exists, and too often doing the right thing ends in heartache and disappointment. But the right thing is the right thing. People do the right thing all the time, and it ends up costing them dearly. Examples include so many throughout history who have stood up against oppression only to be excluded, harmed, or killed.

It certainly is a good practice to listen to the voices of people you trust, and it is also good practice to judge future actions on past experiences. But many times doing the right thing does not require the approval of those around us or the perceived success of the results. Doing what the masses want has created more harm throughout history than any of us would like to admit. There are a lot of "successful" people and businesses in this world who gained their success by hurting and oppressing others. The bottom line of their business does not determine the success of their lives or the purity of their hearts. Better to end life penniless and friendless with a trail of goodness than to have a packed house full of people who feel obligated to be there.

15

Inclusivity

Our ability to reach unity in diversity will be
the beauty and the test of our civilization.
—Mahatma Gandhi

AFTER A CHURCH SERVICE WHERE I was speaking, a young man
came up to me and asked if he could set up a time to talk. He looked
to be in his early twenties and presented himself very well, which is
a bit of a rarity in my life. I have to admit that I was excited for a bit
of a change of pace. I had gotten so used to talking with addicts,
inmates, and homeless people that the thought of spending time
with a young person who appeared to have his life together sounded
awfully refreshing. I naturally assumed that he was inspired by my
commitment to people living on the margins of society and wanted
to share with me his similar passion. I was excited to share my
boundless wisdom to help set him on his adventurous course of
standing for justice and being a voice for the voiceless. I understand
how egotistical that sounds as I am writing it, but I am no super-
man. Sometimes I simply desire a sense of normalcy, which for me
is rooted in growing up a part of a nice middle-class family with
supportive parents and a community that was always willing to be
my biggest cheerleader and encourager. Well, you know what they

say about assumptions; they make an ass out of you and me—and this story wouldn't be in this book if it played out the way I thought it would.

I set up a meeting with this young man for later the same week and was genuinely excited when he showed up for our appointment. In my line of work, people have not always been good at keeping their commitments. We made ourselves comfortable in my office and started with some small-talk. He grew up in a family not unlike my own, did well in school, and all that. I was gently massaging the conversation, preparing myself for all the wisdom I would have the opportunity to bestow. He then paused before asking, "Matt, can I tell you something?" I noticed when he asked this he started fidgeting and rubbing his hands together. When I noticed this, I thought what any compassionate, well-meaning man of the cloth would think: *Oh, shit.* Against my better judgment I said a word that has gotten me into more awkward conversations than I could ever begin to tell you: "Sure."

The young man looked me in the eyes and shared that what he was about to tell me, he had not told anyone else in his life other than his parents and his therapist. I assured him by saying, "You are free to tell me anything you want. At this point I have heard pretty much everything and nothing you say will likely surprise me." As if the universe took these words as a challenge, he continued. This young man shared with me how he is a regular viewer of *SportsCenter* on ESPN. I said, "We have something in common because I too enjoy watching ESPN." That was the end of our similarities for the day. He then went on to share with me how a year or so earlier the hosts of *SportsCenter* began talking to him directly through his television. He said that Chris Berman and the rest of the crew were telling him secret messages through the broadcasts. And then he went on to share with me some of the craziest things I have ever heard come out of someone's mouth. He felt as if he was getting prophetic messages from God directly from the anchors of *SportsCenter*.

Now, just to be clear, I am the most easygoing, level-headed, poker-faced listener you can imagine. At this point I had a lot of experience hearing really crazy stories. In many of those cases, I would just pray for the appropriate words to respond with. But in this case the only thought going through my head was, *For the love of God do not crack a smile. Do not smile. Don't you dare smile.* Of course his first question afterward was, "You think I'm crazy, don't you?" As a general rule, I make it a standard practice not to lie when I meet with people, but this was a no-win situation. If I say the truth, he walks out; and if I lie, I am not sure I am doing the right thing. So I responded in textbook therapist talk by saying, "I believe that you believe this is true." Well, that didn't go too well. He saw through me and quickly shut down as I was trying to ask questions to discover if he was getting the appropriate mental health assistance he seemed to need. He quickly lumped me into the same group as his parents and therapist and kindly dismissed himself. I never saw him again.

Up to this point, I prided myself on my ability to see people as human beings. I worked very hard to not allow people's current situation, appearance, or even smell to keep me from caring for and loving them equally. It turns out that even though I can do this in situations where many others cannot, when it came down to it, I ended up being just as much of an ass as anyone. I assumed this young man was whole, complete, and without some of the deep challenges that the world tends to hand so many. My assumptions kept me from being present and kept me from developing a helpful relationship with this young man—one that would have connected him to a community that genuinely cared for and loved him. Instead, he left with more shame, more judgment, and more condemnation.

Very few if any of us escape the reality that we are most comfortable with people like ourselves. Our closest friends tend to be a lot like us. They live in similar neighborhoods, value similar things, and even make a similar amount of money. This naturally bleeds into our faith communities, into our workplaces, and into our cities and towns. Spaces in our world that are multicultural and economically diverse are hard to come by.

We live in a world with a horrific underbelly of racism, sexism, and just about every other -ism we can think of. These realities have, historically speaking, given us a head start in our desire for likeness. But if we are honest, we have grabbed onto what we inherited and accepted it as the truth. The minute I think I am above this, I drive through a poor neighborhood and feel my heartrate rise, letting me know that I am just as much at fault as anyone. In the same way I can tell I am a part of the problem when I feel more comfortable sitting with the aforementioned young man who looked like me than I do with the person living on the street or the person who is incarcerated.

For years I did a great job of pointing my finger at churches, religious leaders, and organizations, and rightfully so. I have seen with my own eyes a homeless man be removed from a church service for looking homeless. I have seen firsthand a woman get a talking-to for wearing a V-neck that plunged a bit too far for the comfort of the leadership. I have sat with a man in tears who was not allowed in a church with his court-ordered chaperone because he was a sex offender. I have watched mothers be escorted to rooms with televisions because their kids were too loud. I sat in a meeting where a twenty-year-old young man was fired because of his struggle with pornography. And I am humiliated to admit that I did nothing to help. In every one of those situations I was simply a bystander who chose not to act or to even simply stand with those who were being wronged. So yes, those churches, pastors, and leaders are to blame, but so am I.

The first thing Jesus did when he started his work on earth was gather up some people who are often referred to as disciples. He seemed purposed in his choices. He chose a wide variety of people. The male authors of the Bible created a narrative that he chose twelve men, but I believe that to be shortsighted based on the importance of the many women we see throughout his life. Jesus chose men and women. He chose Jews and zealots. He chose the poor and he chose the rich. He chose the powerful and he chose the powerless. And as he journeyed through his life, he refused any pressures or temptations to treat some better than others. He took time to speak to religious leaders and royalty, and he took time to speak with heathens and the poor. The prostitute was no less and no more important to Jesus than the rich young ruler. The leper was no less and no more important than the priest.

During my time as a prison chaplain I would bring in several pastors from varying traditions to speak, and over seven years and hundreds of church services, I can remember just one sermon. It was from a fiery young Pentecostal preacher who carried a handkerchief, which, side note, is without a doubt the most disgusting invention ever. Thanks to Grandpa Lenny I always get a little queasy when I see a square piece of white cloth. And then to just stick it back in your pocket. Come on! I digress. This young preacher yelled so much that every time he was done his voice was gone. One day he came into a gym full of convicts. There were Native Americans, African Americans, Mexican Americans, Asian Americans, and European Americans all together for an hour. Hundreds of men hanging on his every word and encouraging him every time he banged on the pulpit or stomped his foot. Then, in the middle of his rant, he looked up at this group of about three hundred men of every color and background and said ten words I will never forget. It was one of the very few moments when he wasn't yelling. He looked at them all sitting in a horseshoe on metal bleachers and said, "The ground is level at the foot of the cross." The room went silent, and he paused for a few seconds. Then he yelled it at the top of his lungs while stomping his feet, and the place erupted in applause, amens, whoops, and hollers.

The ground is indeed level at the foot of the cross. Love, grace, and forgiveness are available to all of us, no matter our race, gender, sexual orientation, or anything else. I believe with all my heart that the ground is level at the foot of the cross, but I am equally confident that the terrain is rocky and varied under my feet. In my world some people get to stand on higher ground than others, and if I am brutally honest, there are many times when I dig holes to ensure that the ground for some remains low. And my heart is a microcosm of our world.

I sincerely hope that you are not like me, but I am fairly confident that on some level you are. A little while ago I looked back at the podcast guests I've had over the previous couple of months and realized they were all men, they were all well put together professionals, and all but one of them were white. I then looked at my bookshelf to find a bunch of books written by a bunch of white men and women. I glanced at my Spotify playlist only to see far more white artists than people of color. I checked my Netflix history, and most of the main characters on the shows I watched were white. I checked my Facebook friends and followers—more white people. I checked my phone contacts—less than ten people of color. And finally I looked to my right and to my left, and what did I see? A bunch of middle-class white people. I have fought for justice my whole life and have worked to give a voice to the voiceless my entire career, and yet I look down to see a ground full of hills and valleys. The people on the hills look and act like me and those in the valleys don't. It's that simple. Why should I expect the ground to be level in churches or in my city or in my country if it is not even level right in front of me? And the worst part is that the person who stands on one of the highest parts of the topography . . . is usually me.

So every day I wake up and grab my shovel, hoping for the opportunity to build up a bit of dirt in one of the valleys to raise up a person I have put down. I don't go around looking for people of color, or people who are gay, or people who are poor to be friends with. I just keep my shovel over my shoulder, prepared for any opportunity that presents itself. I do, however, seek out authors with different backgrounds than me, interviews with people who don't think like me, shows and music from creators who don't look like me. I have no dream of accomplishing what Jesus did, but I am certainly hopeful that the ground at my feet will become a little more like Iowa and a bit less like Colorado.

Bring It Home

As you continue on the journey of life and faith, it is likely that you will discover fewer absolutes and less certainty than you once had. I think for the most part this is a good reality. But there is a space where absolutes are good and necessary and where certainty is vital. That is the space of equality. For faith to matter for anyone, it has to matter for everyone. If I were to pick one reason I walked away from organized religion, it is because the grace that was touted was conditional and the love that was taught as perfect was anything but.

The divine must absolutely be for everyone. It may look different from person to person, but if it is worth anything, it must be available to everyone. I am certain I have work to do in this area. Not because I intentionally look at some people as better than others, but because I unintentionally do, based on the life I have lived. Faith and humanity at their best are inclusive. Faith and humanity at their worst decide who is in and who is out.

16

Forgiveness

Forgiveness is the fragrance that the violet sheds
on the heel that has crushed it.
—Attributed to Mark Twain

MY WIFE AND I WERE music directors at a large church just outside of Minneapolis for a short time. Although the experience was
less than great, we sure did enjoy the quality of talent available.
I'll never forget the day when the keyboard player for Prince (yes,
that Prince) came up after a service to ask if he could be a part of
the worship team. It's safe to say that we skipped the formalities
of an audition process. The best part was that, in true pop star
form, he showed up for the first service in a button-up see-through
mesh shirt. Although I have seen nipples on statues of Jesus, this
was the first and most likely the last time I ever saw real-life nipples in church.

One day while leading music, I remember standing onstage,
looking over the thousand or so people in attendance, and thinking,
All these people look the same. Nearly all were white, they dressed the
same, they probably made about the same amount of money, and the
parking lot was filled with very nice cars, most of which were either
Mercedes or BMWs. In that moment I realized that my quest to find

God had led me to a place that could not look more unlike the ragtag bunch of people Jesus surrounded himself with. For that reason and for many others, including a lead pastor who told my wife she had nice legs, we waltzed into that pastor's office and resigned. There was no plan in place. We just knew we didn't want to be a part of a place that felt more like a country club than a place of worship. Gone were the great musicians, the nice salary, and the ridiculous budget, and gained was a part of my soul—the part that desired a more diverse and beautiful kind of faith community.

In hindsight, since I was a husband and a father of two with a mortgage, it may have been wise to find a job before quitting a job, but honestly, that's just not how I operate. I spent months trying to locate employment in a space that would include the types of people Jesus liked to hang out with. I applied at homeless shelters, charter schools for kids who struggled in normal settings, and finally, at the urging of a friend, I applied at a medium-security prison for a chaplain position. Jesus said that the way we treat prisoners is the way we treat him (Matthew 25:34-40), so I figured it was worth a shot. For an excruciating three-month period all I received was silence. Not a single request for an interview. Time and money were running out when, after a short getaway trip with my parents and the family, I came home, looked at the house I built but no longer could afford, and opened the mailbox. Inside was a single envelope from the medium-security prison. I opened it and found an interview request.

Up to this point I had been in a prison two times, both intentionally. Once was on a mission trip to Mexico and the other was to play drums for a worship band in Minneapolis. The second of those experiences was unbelievably powerful; I was able to experience what it was like when people who had nothing to gain showed up to

sing in spite of their dire situations. The singing was more like shout-
ing, and there was a sense that these men really believed they needed
God. The best word to describe it was *desperation*.

I sat in the interview with two men in uniforms and a very serious looking woman. They did not smile a single time, and for most
of the interview their heads were down as they tediously scribbled
notes. I was well aware that the only thing I had going for me was my
wit, charm, and solid eye contact since I had no formal training to be
a chaplain and no experience working in a correctional setting. That
wit and charm was a no-go since the emotional depth in the room
seemed lacking, and I was not even sure any convincing eye contact
was going to happen since they were not looking at me. I can't
remember any of the questions, but I do remember scanning the
three of them, waiting for even the smallest glance so I could catch
their eyes, which I did a few times with each. Either my plan worked,
or I was the only option available because less than a week later I was
officially back on the employment train.

I received my breakaway lanyard that was made to snap off if
someone tried to choke me (comforting thought) along with a bunch
of keys, and I was ushered through some really loud metal doors into
a sally port where I was held to confirm my identity. A couple months
later, after getting dreadlocks, I was held in this same sally port on
my way out of work because the security guard thought I was an
inmate trying to escape. Apparently dreadlocks are more likely to be
on an inmate than an employee. Eventually a more seasoned guard
came and confirmed that I was indeed the chaplain. I was given no
training other than some basic HR nonsense until several months
into the job and was left to pretty much figure things out for myself
with the help of the other two seasoned chaplains who worked there.
The chapel was on the far side of the property, so my first experience

included walking past the rec yard as hundreds of inmates stared down the new skinny white Polish guy strolling into town.

For the first several months working there, many of the men wanted to spend time with me one-on-one just to introduce themselves and often to share their stories. This one-on-one time was something I continued to do for the entirety of the seven years I worked there. To this day that office is one of the most sacred, life-altering places of my existence. There were tears shed over regrets and over the loss of loved ones. There were intense conversations about life, during which all I could do was pray, because I didn't know what I was supposed to say to a man weeping over the fact that he had murdered his wife, to a man begging God to be able to see his kids, to a man who didn't understand his attraction to children, or to a man who just found out that his mother passed away knowing that the only option he had to say his goodbyes was a private video viewing of the funeral. In these situations words felt lacking and faith was about all I had. This was the time when I truly discovered that listening is the most powerful tool available to a human being, because even though answers were hard to find inside those prison walls, the opportunity to be heard proved healing for many.

One day a twenty-one-year-old man was milling around by my office door, glancing at me from time to time. After a few minutes of this I simply asked him if he needed something, which he heard as an invitation to come on in and have a seat. He was full of energy, vibrant, and friendly. This young man was known as a short-timer since his sentence was only a few years long and he was being held at this medium-security prison only until a spot became available for him at a minimum-security facility. John sat down and immediately began sharing his story, his hopes, and his dreams with me. He was extremely pleasant, and I sincerely enjoyed our time together.

Shortly after that first conversation, I received a request from John to meet again, which I was happy to do. This time when he arrived, that infectious spirit seemed a bit muted. He asked if it was okay for him to share his childhood experience with me. I assured him that I was more than willing to listen. John shared that from as far back as he could remember, his father would come home drunk and beat him. He told me that it wasn't just any beating with hands, fists, or even a belt. His father's weapon of choice was a two-by-four. For those of you unfamiliar with what that is, it is a piece of solid construction wood that gets the name from its measurement in inches. It has no give, and it is very difficult to break. It is thick enough to be the primary thing that likely holds up the house or apartment you live in. With tears in his eyes John told me that day after day, month after month, year after year, he was beaten regularly by his father. He told me that the beatings finally stopped when he was sixteen years old and his father tried to hit him for a final time. John was finally strong enough to grab the piece of lumber and rip it away from his dad's clenched hands. This, he informed me, was the last time he was ever beaten, and it was also the last time he ever saw his father. He cried while I listened and told him how proud I was of him for sharing openly and for still being able to live with hope and optimism for the future because something like that would ruin most of us. Yet here he was, living around a bunch of felons, bringing light and energy into the chapel every time he walked in.

About a week later John was once again at my door with all that energy and optimism restored. He sat down and told me that since our last conversation, he had spent a lot of time thinking about his childhood and his father, and because of his newfound faith in God he was trying to discover what God would desire him to do with his story and with his father. John told me that he was praying when an idea came to him. He said, "Chap, I am going to write my dad a letter." I encouraged him that if writing a letter was what he felt prompted to do, he should do it. I told him I would be happy to read the letter before he sent it if that would be helpful. After another week went by, John was at my door, this time with a letter in his hand. I unfolded the two sheets of paper he handed me and was immediately moved by the kind and loving words I read. There was not a hint of anger in his writing. The entire letter reached a crescendo on the final page when he wrote, "Dad, I forgive you." I looked up at John with tears in my eyes and my heart beating fast. But that was not the end of the story, only the beginning.

Later that day John sent out the letter, which in and of itself would have been enough to free him from the bonds of anger and bitterness he had been holding onto. Another week passed before John came flying back into the chapel, straight to my office door, holding an envelope in his hand. He reached out and placed in my hand a letter from his father. I opened it and was awestruck by what was enclosed. It was a story of regret and pain. John's father wrote of how he was so ashamed and filled with guilt that he couldn't find it in his heart to locate his son and ask for forgiveness because he feared that it was simply not an option. At the end of the letter he asked if he could come and visit his son. I sat there silently for a few minutes, trying to digest the story that was unfolding in front of me. I handed the letter back to John. I assured him that no one would fault him if this was just too much. I said that forgiveness does not need to include allowing an abuser back into your life. John looked me in the eyes as if he heard nothing I said and told me that he was going to send his father a visiting form.

The visiting form was approved the day before John's dad showed up at the facility. I called to check in with him. John came to my office all smiles as usual. I shared with him that tomorrow was likely going to be a very emotional day. I asked John to close his eyes and visualize the moment when his father walked into the visiting room. The moment when the man who beat him with a piece of lumber for most of his life, until John physically stopped him just five years prior, would walk back into his life. I asked him, "What are you going to do when you see him?" John opened his eyes, slowly stood up, and opened his arms wide for an embrace. "I am going to give my dad a hug," he said. "That's what I am going to do. I'm going to give him a hug."

The next day, John's father showed up, and John did exactly what he said he was going to do. He embraced his father in an act of love and grace unlike anything I had ever seen before that moment.

When I read the Bible passage about the treatment of prisoners being a direct reflection of my relationship with Jesus, I assumed that meant I was to serve inmates and therefore serve Jesus. That was not my experience at all. My experience was that by taking the time to listen, I was able to learn lessons life had been unable to teach me up to that point. What I learned is that grace is more real, alive, and dynamic than I ever thought possible. It's not so much about serving Jesus, prisoners, or the oppressed, but about listening and learning from them. How arrogant was I to assume otherwise?

After spending most of my life surrounded by people who looked and acted a lot like me, for seven years I was blessed to be in the minority (which is another problem for another book). Everyone came from somewhere different, and I could look around and feel as if I was starting to learn how to truly love Jesus for the first time. There was only one option for a worship service each weekend, and whatever it was, everyone attended. The Charismatics came to the Lutheran service and the Lutherans returned the favor. One week we would sing gospel music and the next week we would open our hymnals. Things that matter in our churches on the outside did not matter in the chapel. Preachers were not concerned about offerings, and no one bothered to act holier than thou because the worst moments of their lives were on full display by the color of their outfits and by the fact that they were identified more by a number assigned to them by the Department of Corrections than by their actual name. After decades in church buildings, after hundreds of worship services and sermons, a twenty-one-year-old inmate named John was finally able to show me what grace looks like.

Bring It Home

As we walk away from people and places that taught us "spiritual truths," we can rest assured that lessons about the divine can be learned in buildings without crosses from people without collars or seminary degrees. Life itself is the true spiritual teacher if we are open to the lessons.

My friend Craig Scott, a school shooting victim who lost his sister in the Columbine High School tragedy and watched two of his friends get shot and killed right next to him under a table in the library, once shared with me that "forgiveness is like setting a prisoner free and then finding out that prisoner is you." We can walk away from the church, from organized religion, or from Evangelicalism and the like, but we need to continue to walk toward forgiveness even when it is hard and even when it doesn't make much sense. On our search for faith we may need to discover how to forgive those who taught us about forgiveness in the first place.

As we journey back home, it is tempting to distance ourselves from everything associated with that thing that was hard and hurtful. I often see people respond to struggle by swinging the pendulum far over to the opposite side. I can completely understand why this is the case, and I believe it can even be helpful. As we create space between ourselves and toxic beliefs and patterns, we should also hold tight to the part of our faith that has been meaningful and life-changing. The power of forgiveness is something we will benefit from only if we are willing to allow ourselves the freedom to take hold of it.

17

Hope

It's better to light a candle than to curse the darkness.
—Eleanor Roosevelt

EVERY GENERATION HAS A HANDFUL of moments when everyone can remember where they were. For my generation, this includes the collapse of the twin towers on 9/11 and now the storming of the Capitol in 2021. For my parents it includes the assassination of JFK and MLK, and for my grandparents it was the bombing of Pearl Harbor. Inside these big events we all remember there are other events more specific to who we are. For me, one of those events was the tragic shooting at Columbine High School when two boys entered a school with semiautomatic weapons and homemade bombs and opened fire, killing twelve students, one teacher, and themselves.

I was in my final semester of college, studying to be a music teacher, and in the middle of my internship at a middle school. I was walking through the foyer of the school when they put the Columbine footage on television screens and made several announcements about what was happening. I remember standing there staring at the television, unable to comprehend all I was seeing and having no clue the extent to which this would change our culture and our education system. For many of us, this was the first time we began to wonder, *If even our schools are not safe, what is?*

After graduation I landed my first interview and became an official high school band director. This was a far cry from my dream job, but since I had the degree and no other great options for supporting my new wife, mortgage, car, and dog, it seemed like a good idea in the moment. I have to admit that having my very own health insurance and retirement plan felt pretty good for a minute. I was suddenly in the world of adulting.

Adulting, it turns out, didn't fit me very well, and less than six months into my teaching contract I let the principal know that this would be a one-and-done. I loved being with teenagers, but listening to out-of-tune clarinets and oboes and obnoxious percussionists was not my idea of a future. I gave up the job and the insurance. We sold nearly every possession we had, including our house, and we even found a new home for the dog so we could travel around the country in a 1995 Dodge Caravan, playing music anywhere people would listen. For nearly two years we didn't have an actual address, and for all I know we were included in homeless statistics for our community. At this point in life I was starting to learn the pieces that didn't fit. Even though we had no end goal in mind, we were quite literally driving away from what wasn't working and toward something that seemed to make more sense. Strange how being homeless without a plan in a minivan full of music equipment could make more sense than a solid job with a steady paycheck and a home to call our own, but it most certainly did. We didn't engage in a single conversation, at any point, about going back.

Everything leads to the next thing, and that is the story of my life. Even though I didn't end up sticking it out as an educator, I did manage to use the skills I acquired as a communicator in most of the positions I have held. Eventually I started becoming known for this ability. For much of my life being a drummer was my identity, and it was the thing I was most known for. Slowly but surely that began to change to the point where now many of the people I am around have no idea that I am a musician.

It started when we needed to fill some time during concerts and no one else wanted to stand in front and talk. Then my pastor wanted me to speak about worship music in church. That was the moment I realized that people found me funny as hell. I'll never forget standing in front of five hundred people who were laughing so hard I couldn't get them to stop. And this was during a church sermon. I have no idea what I said, but the ability to bring laughter and joy felt amazing! After that I was invited to speak for a breakout session at a youth camp, which led to me being one of their primary speakers for years. From there I went to a medium-security prison where I surprised even myself to find out that I was good enough to hold a room full of inmates captive (that's the one dad joke I get for this book) for forty-five minutes at a time.

The universe has a beautiful way of keeping us humble, and when I planted and pastored our beautiful little community for those living in the margins of our city, people regularly slept through my messages, answered their phones, and struck up loud conversations. On really special days, the police would show up just when I was really getting revved up to see if a crime suspect was hanging out with us. They usually were. An arrest is a real buzzkill during a sermon.

Eventually, speaking in evangelical Christian circles became something I could no longer do while still being able to look at myself in the mirror. Even though I refused to speak any messages of exclusion, representing any organization that did made me guilty by association. The problem was, it such a natural fit for what I was good at. I would sit quietly by myself often, wondering if life as a public speaker was over for good. A friend of mine who used to be a national youth speaker and a megachurch speaking pastor before leaving the evangelical world said to me once, "It's like I'm a speaker without a venue." I was not comfortable believing that part of my life was over, and still to this day it is something I crave. I love doing it more than anything else in the world, so I did what anyone in my shoes would do in the same situation. I hopped on the computer and went to Indeed.com. In the search engine I typed in "motivational speaker." When it asked where I wanted to work, I simply typed "United States." There was a single match that came up, and it was for an organization out of Littleton, Colorado, called Rachel's Challenge.

I read the description and headed to their website where I read a story about a seventeen-year-old girl at Columbine High School in Littleton, Colorado, who was the first of twelve students killed in what is often viewed as the first mass school shooting in U.S. history. Suddenly I was transported back to that moment in history when I was standing at the very beginning of my career journey, stunned by this very event. And now nearly twenty years later I was staring at a possibility to be a part of the solution.

I knew it was a long shot since it was a national search for just a couple of spots, but after talking with their HR director, I submitted my application along with my audition video. Three months later I was on a plane heading out to Colorado to be trained as a speaker for Rachel's Challenge.

The first year with the organization was nothing short of exhilarating and inspiring. After her death, Rachel's father, Darrell Scott, committed his life to continuing the chain reaction of kindness and compassion that his daughter started when she was alive. He didn't take up a crusade against gun violence or bullying; instead, he uses Rachel's life story to inspire students and adults all over the nation and world to simply care for one another. Even though the portion of our presentation about the school shooting is difficult to watch and the loss of fifteen lives is tragic and horrific to hear about, the tears at the end of the presentation are never because of Rachel's death, but because of her life. The tears at the end of the presentation are because those present realize the power they have to change the lives of those around them by simply being kind and compassionate.

Darrell Scott made one decision that changed the lives of millions of people throughout the world. He made a decision that I am not sure I would be capable of if I were in his shoes. He decided to be *for* something instead of *against* something. If we are going to oppose something, we should also know what we would like to see instead. Jesus didn't speak much about what he was against, but he spoke a great deal about what he was for.

One of the greatest challenges of leaving the evangelical world and leaving church is that people often feel relieved and lost at the same time. The most common thing I hear from those who have left is that they feel a great deal of freedom while at the same time feeling a great deal of sadness and anger. I'll never forget the feeling I had when I was asked to leave B-Side, the community I started, because of what I believed. I walked out the door with a huge smile on my face and with a deep desire to punch a wall. The sadness comes from the reality that we all loved it so much at one point in time. It defined us, gave us hope, allowed us to feel love. We built our entire lives inside those walls, and now, standing on the outside, we feel the deep reality of the divorce. And for those of us who worked in churches or served in churches, we wonder if we will ever find a way or even the strength to do what we love to do again. The anger comes from realizing that we all bought into a lie. A lie that we were right and everyone else was wrong. A lie that we had the corner on the truth. In reality, it is just a toxic machine that is ruining our world.

Religion has become good at being against things and people when all Jesus desired was togetherness. The word he used during the only documented time he prayed was *unity* (John 17)—that we would be for each other and with each other in the same way he and his Father are for each other and with each other. The church has historically preached a message of division. If you are on the inside, and you serve, give, and believe correctly, you will receive all the benefits it has to give. But as soon as you don't fit or you question the foundation on which it is built, you are no longer allowed to be a beneficiary. Several prominent authors who have written and spoken messages that go against the grain have been publicly excommunicated from the church after being its poster children for decades.

The thing we loved about being a part of the church does exist and is very much alive outside of it. True community should not be defined by having the same beliefs, but by having similar hearts. What many of us experienced was, for the most part, a cheap substitution for something that is real and beautiful. It's like saying sex with a prostitute is true intimacy. It's not! The moment you stop paying, it goes away. In the same way many church gatherings do not represent true community because when you leave, you lose. I don't think I have met a single person who has left the church without losing most of their friends.

We certainly have to take the time to grieve our loss. For me this was a three-year process where I took a job as an activities director at an elder care home because I needed to be in a place where people didn't care about my faith beliefs, where I could offer some value without worrying about eternal damnation. By the third year I started feeling less angry and less sad. When I became less angry and sad, I started to become more curious and determined. There had to be a way to be involved with something that looks more like Jesus than the church. There had to be a path to get back to doing what I love and what I am good at in a way that is inclusive, beautiful, and meaningful. There had to be a way to engage in community and friendship that didn't hinge on my beliefs. The last part was easy. I looked at my life and identified the handful of people who were still there and realized that they had always been there. My only mistake was not realizing it earlier. I've always had true community! I have just been choosing a false substitute. The second part started with believing in myself enough to send in my resume and audition video for Rachel's Challenge, and it also started with the bravery to come out as a heretic through my podcast, erasing any doubt about my views and beliefs!

These steps led to other opportunities. I now create content and speak for an anti-trafficking organization called Fierce Freedom, and I have had the opportunity to help many people get their voices out into the world by producing and cohosting podcasts with them. Within two years of sending in my resume to Rachel's Challenge, I managed to carve out a career that feeds every space in my soul. I get to do what I love in a way that looks more beautiful and godly than anything in the church ever did. I decided never to work for or with a "Christian" organization again, and through that decision I've found people who look like Jesus, act like Jesus, and love like Jesus. I have found organizations who are doing Jesus-like work in this world by standing up for the oppressed and by speaking life and love. The community of friends I have always love me no matter what. They love things about me that drive most other people nuts. They laugh with me, they check in with me, they ask me how I am doing.

And although relationships don't come naturally to me, I am trying to offer the same value for them.

The work I now am honored to be a part of in this world is work for people, for justice, for love, and for beauty. The lesson I learned from Darrell Scott after he tragically lost his daughter is one that will drive me for the rest of my life. It is amazing what can be accomplished when we choose to be *for* instead of *against*. And here is the great thing: when people hear what I am for, they also know what I am against. If you know that I am for total inclusion for everyone no matter what, you also know I am against any sort of exclusion, so you don't have to ask me if I think being gay is a sin. If you know that I am for peace, you also know that I am against violence, so you don't have to ask me where I stand on private ownership of military grade weapons. If you know that I am for life, you also know that I am against death, so you don't have to ask me where I stand on capital punishment.

There is life after the church. This is a big world, and there is space for all of us. There are needs in this world, and you have what is needed to meet some of those needs. You are not a speaker without a venue, a musician without a stage, or a host without a front door. Your options didn't get eliminated by the exclusion of church; they get expanded. Go find your venue! Go find your stage! Open the front door to possibilities. As author Leonard Sweet wrote in *Aqua Church*, "The church began to die when the first wall was built." By walking toward life, you will naturally walk away from death!

After I presented for Rachel's Challenge at an event in Pennsylvania, a young woman approached me with a journal in her hands. She thanked me for being there and flipped to the front of her journal. She looked me in the eyes and said, "In the front on this journal are all of the reasons I didn't believe I should be on this earth; all of the reasons that I was going to kill myself." She then flipped to the back of the journal and continued, "After hearing Rachel's story, I decided I want to live, and these are all of the reasons I belong here and all of the reasons I need to be alive." That is what is possible when we are brave enough to worry less about what we are against and decide what it is we are for!

Bring It Home

Most of you reading this book have gone through very difficult situations regarding church and faith. The reason you are looking for a change is that you have found enough wrong with what you were a part of.

It is important to find time and space to talk through the hurts and disappointments you experienced. It is equally important to stop talking about them at some point so you can move forward in a healthy and meaningful way. Believe me when I say that this is much easier said than done, and we have to be careful not to rush the process. Some are able move forward quickly, with an almost supernatural ability to forgive and see with new perspective. For others like myself, it was and in some ways still is a long and grueling journey, filled with a lot of anger, frustration, hurt, and disappointment. Through my healing process one lesson I have learned is that the longer we hold onto the hurt and disappointment, the longer it holds onto us.

There are a lot of spaces in the faith-deconstruction world that can only be described as platforms to complain. Again, that certainly has its place for a while, until it just gets old. What is important is not so much what we are running away from, but what we are walking toward.

18

Intentions

You've got to know what you want.
This is central to acting on your intentions.
—From the movie *Patch Adams*

THE BEST PART ABOUT BEING a prison chaplain was all the incredible men I had the opportunity to meet. And let me assure you, none of these incredible men worked for the prison. They were all incarcerated. We often have this impression that people in prison are hard, troubled humans who are dangerous and not all that pleasant to be around. To be honest, there were most certainly plenty of these people in the prison where I worked, but most of the men I had the pleasure to meet were kind, loving, passionate, and purposed. If we were all judged by our worst moments—you know, that thing no one else knows about—if that was exposed to the world and everyone judged you based on it, I am guessing you wouldn't have the greatest reputation either. To give you an example, there was a young man serving a life sentence because he got drunk when he was a teenager, got behind the wheel, crashed his car, and killed three of his closest friends. That is a horrible moment he has been paying for ever since. But it doesn't define who he is because he is a kind and warm-hearted man who was a true joy to be around.

Maybe it was his amazing dreadlocks or his biceps that were as large as my waist, but there was one man whom I connected with in a special way. His name was Roderick, and I met him when I hired him to be one of the chapel clerks. In most prison systems the inmates have opportunities to work in various positions throughout the facility. It's a win-win scenario because the incarcerated men get some work experience and make a little money while the prison gets some cheap labor out of the deal. The best jobs paid a whopping one dollar an hour, but keep in mind that all housing, meals, and medical is covered by our tax dollars, so they don't have a lot of costs to cover. Most men would keep some money out for snacks, save some for their release, and send some home to help out family. The chapel clerk was responsible for keeping track of library books and checking men in and out of the chapel along with any other tasks that I or the other two chaplains had for him.

My regular shift at the prison ended at 9:00 p.m. after all the evening activities were finished. Roderick worked in the evenings, and because he was a dedicated worker, he would often finish his responsibilities before the end of my shift. When this happened, I would often invite him into my office and we would talk, not as chaplain to inmate, but as friends. Over time I would say we not only became friends, but we became really good friends. From a Department of Corrections standpoint this is simply not allowed. But when I began the position, I made a pact with myself that I was going to do what I felt was right no matter what. Because of this pact, I naturally assumed that my time would end by getting walked out (a phrase that means you get your ass fired). If I have learned one thing in my forty-plus years of existence, it is to be careful with what you claim as the truth, because for better or worse, it often comes to be.

Rod and I would talk about life, faith, family, and all sorts of things. It was an amazing relationship between two people who were not supposed to be friends. I was the chaplain; he was the inmate. I am white; he is Black. I grew up in rural Wisconsin; he grew up in Milwaukee. I am tall and skinny; he is short and built like a house. I would tell him that if people saw us walking down the street, they would think we were the number ten.

Roderick was a teenager when he agreed to be a part of an armed robbery. He didn't have or hold a gun, yet he ended up with twenty years in prison. I personally know people who have done much more serious crimes and have served much less time. The prison system, my friends, is beyond messed up and is in desperate need of reform. When I met him, his entire adult life had been lived inside the walls of a prison.

At one point in our conversations, Rod explained to me that he had a desire to begin advocating for himself and others whom he felt were being imprisoned for far more time than what seemed fair or logical. He discovered a nonprofit organization that was fighting for prison reform in our state and decided to write the organization a letter to see if his experience inside the system as an inmate would be helpful to their efforts. He asked me to read his letter before he sent it, which I was happy to do. After proofreading it for him, I clicked print on my computer so he could stick it in the mail.

The following day I came to work and, for the first time since I hired him, Rod did not show up for his shift. This was concerning since he was a very reliable worker, so I picked up my phone and called down to his unit to see what was going on. The officer who answered informed me that he had been locked up in segregation, which means he got in trouble for something. Segregation is where inmates go who are accused of a major rule violation. They are forced to spend a period of time in a cell by themselves, without the freedoms of the general population. For the entire time I worked at the prison, Rod had not once been in any sort of trouble. I was obviously concerned, and since chapel activities had not yet started for the evening, I walked over to the segregation unit to see what happened. When I arrived, I headed over to his cell. He looked at me through the door and simply said, "Chap, they found the letter." It turned out that after printing the letter for Rod, we ended up talking some more, and I left it sitting on the staff printer. This was a problem because staff members were not allowed to print things for inmates.

The next day I was scheduled for work, I walked in and there was a senior security officer waiting for me at my office door. I was interrogated as if I were some sort of hardened criminal. There was a very angry man in a white shirt asking all sorts of questions, and there was another man also in a white shirt typing furiously on his computer recording my responses. The basic questions were fine, but then I was asked, "Do you have compassion for the inmates here?" To which I responded, "I'm pretty sure that is what you hired me for." Because of my original intention of staying true to my convictions, the pressed white uniform did not intimidate me one bit. And because I knew the man questioning me to be an absolute ass who prided himself on taking people down, I knew he was expecting me to cower to his authority. Instead, I sat on the edge of my chair, leaned forward, and stared in his eyes the entire time. I informed him how I believed the entire system we worked for was a pile of shit. I told him that we were working in a system where if we succeed and men leave and don't come back, then we are out of our jobs. So in a sense we are incentivized to help these men fail. I informed him that his aggression was not helpful, but instead was a major part of the problem. Every time I challenged him I could see his face grow new shades of red. And I'm not going to lie, I was having at least a little bit of fun. Worst-case scenario, he walks me out, which I expected eventually. Best-case scenario, he actually listens to something I had to say. The interrogation culminated in the moment the officer said, "Today you print a letter for him; tomorrow you bring in a gun for him." To which I replied, "Well, that feels like a pretty big leap!"

This dance went on for several weeks. Every time I came in to work, I assumed some man in a white shirt would want to ask me more questions. Eventually, one day I showed up and there was yet another man in a white shirt waiting for me by my office door. He told me to grab my belongings because he was "walking me out." During our quarter-mile walk out of the institution he let me know how much he hated this part of his job and that he understood how difficult my position as a chaplain must be. I really appreciated his words. It was one of those rare moments in life when someone seems to understand you on some level. I walked out the door for what I assumed would be the final time and took off my lanyard before hopping in the car. I arrived home several hours early with flowers in hand, announcing, "Daddy's home!"

I patiently waited for the final fatal phone call from the prison, and about a week later, sure enough, the phone rang, and the number was listed as private. I braced myself and hit *accept*, expecting to hear my supervisor or the warden on the other end. Instead, it was an HR representative who informed me that I could return to work the next day. That was certainly unexpected! Apparently they had a change of heart, and they saw the error of their ways.

The following day I headed back to work to the surprise of pretty much everyone there. It was just before Christmas, and the warden was walking around the institution handing out candy canes to the inmates as I made my way to the office. Within an hour my phone rang, and as I picked it up, I heard the voice of the holly jolly warden asking me to come to his office. I was pretty sure this was not a good sign. I hung up the phone and headed to the administrative building. I walked in, and he asked me to have a seat. The warden then launched into a long-winded monologue explaining how he was concerned for me. This was humorous because this was the first conversation we had ever had, and I am at least fairly confident that before this incident he did not even know my name. As he drew his speech to an end, he informed me that I would be getting a month off without pay due to this horrible printout I had made. I simply smiled, asked him for a candy cane, and walked out the door. From there I walked into my supervisor's office, candy cane hanging out of my mouth, and informed her that I was resigning effective one day after my unpaid time off. I had no intention of giving up my incredible health insurance any earlier than I had to. I am not above playing the game to my advantage.

After the month was over, I came to the prison on a Saturday to speak at my final service with the inmates. I have no idea what I said during that message, but I do remember that it was one of the most emotional worship services I have ever been a part of. Men were crying as I spoke, and I too was fighting back tears. And then, as the gospel choir came up to end the service, they asked me to stay up front so they could pray for me. Brother Roy, one of the leaders of the choir, said, "Chaplain, today we are commissioning you out of this prison. We are sending you with our blessing and our prayers as a missionary into the world." Dozens of men from every background, ethnicity, and belief system came forward and put their hands on my shoulders (also not allowed by the Department of Corrections). They prayed over me for several minutes, and I do not believe it will ever be possible to be a part of something more powerful and more beautiful than that moment. As I walked out of the prison for the last time, I took off my lanyard and felt like twenty-pound weights were lifted off my shoulders. After fighting so hard for these men and believing in them so much, after being at odds with the administration for most of my employment, my time at the prison was over. But this story is not.

Every day for nearly a year after I left, I would receive letters from incarcerated men. They shared their gratefulness, asked for prayers, and made sure I had their contact information. I tried feebly to keep up by writing back, but it proved impossible. I did my best to at least respond to the first letter anyone sent and informed them that continued communication would be difficult, but that they would never leave my heart or mind. One day, after several months, I received yet another letter from the Wisconsin prison system. The name on the return address was Roderick Harris.

Rod had been moved to another institution after his time in segregation and shared with me all the crazy things he had to endure as a result of the letter I printed for him. They treated him no differently than a man who stole money from his workplace or who got into a fight. He apologized for any difficulty it caused me and ended by simply expressing his love and gratitude. I immediately wrote back and shared things from my side of the story, also apologizing for all the hardship he had to endure. We remained in contact first by writing letters, and then, after many years, we were able to talk on the phone.

During one of our conversations, Rod paused, got choked up, and informed me that his release date was approaching. After nearly twenty years—his whole adult life—Rod had a date for his release after being a part of a crime in which he didn't hurt anyone and in which he didn't even have a weapon on him. I was beyond excited that he was finally being released twelve years after our first meeting. We spent several phone calls simply preparing him for a place that was going to feel very foreign. At the time over fifty percent of men released in Wisconsin ended up back in prison, and I wanted to do whatever I could to ensure that this would not be Rod's story. We discussed relationships, family, work, friends, and anything else I could think of. Finally, after one of our conversations I asked, "Rod, would you be okay if I came to Milwaukee to be there the moment you walk out of prison a free man?"

At the end of March 2021, I was standing outside a minimum-security prison behind Rod's family and friends and a camera crew, staring at a chain-link fence topped with razor wire. He was scheduled to be released at 9:00 a.m., and that time came and went. Apparently after he gave the state twenty years of his life, they thought it appropriate to make him wait an additional twenty minutes. And then it happened. Out walked this man with a swagger I remembered well, pushing a small cart that held all his earthly belongings. His mother began jumping up and down and eventually ran toward him, at which point Rod yelled, "Mom, don't run! They shoot Black people for that in this country!" It was certainly good to hear that his sense of humor was well intact. As she got closer to him, he let his cart go and embraced his mother for what felt like the better part of eternity. After finally letting her go, he looked everyone in the eye and began to repeat the phrase, "We did it!" Rod went from person to person, hollering, "We did it!" And then gave them an embrace not unlike the one he gave his mother. When it was my turn, I thought he might never let go!

From there we went to a local diner to enjoy his first meal as a free adult man. He responded to every moment like a child on Christmas morning. From being able to order off a menu to being served more food than he could ever dream of eating in one sitting, to getting a bill, pulling out a wad of cash, and offering to pay since he never had that opportunity in his entire life. I didn't let him pick up the tab, but I gladly let him leave as big of a tip as he wanted.

Life since Rod's release has not been without challenges, but he has faced each one with grace, authenticity, and a belief that if he can make it through twenty years in prison, he can make it through whatever life may throw at him as a free man.

Bring It Home

As we journey back home, the path will be filled with temptations to turn around or to do the thing that feels easy in the moment. For me the temptation for years was to go back to the comfortable arms of the church community that rejected me. I know that if I succumb to the pressure and pretend like all my doubts and questions have somehow faded away, open arms would be ready for me. I would be like the prodigal son, and, as you recall, that story ends very well for him. He actually ends up with more than what he left with. My other temptation has been to do what so many before me have done, which is to start a new version of the same thing. Rarely does a week go by when I am not asked to start a progressive Christian church. As alluring as that sounds, history shows that all that would happen is we would struggle with the same things in new ways.

The answers are not as clear as they once seemed, but one thing that is universally true is that if we hang on to our convictions and walk forward in authenticity, desiring to be the truest and most beautiful forms of ourselves, the end result will be something we can be proud of. Not necessarily proud of what we create, or of what we are a part of, but simply proud that we set our intentions and stuck to our convictions.

Roderick is a man who, in spite of being put in a brutally difficult situation, found in the deepest parts of himself peace in the midst of his struggle. Most incarcerated men I've met simply went along with what everyone else was doing. They did what they needed to do in order to feel safe and to fit in. I cannot fault them for doing this, and I cannot pretend that I would have done anything different. We discover what we are made of only when we have the chance to find out what is within us. Rod is a person I look up to because he stood out among the crowd. He didn't buy into the system that was responsible for the high recidivism rate. Instead, he stayed true to himself, and after many long years, it paid off.

If you are reading this book, at some point in your life you likely felt as if you had things figured out regarding God and faith. And now it is quite possible that you are experiencing some significant insecurities that in one moment make you feel free and alive and in the next moment make you feel scared out of your mind. In the midst of this fear and freedom, set your intentions. Why are you here, and what are you hoping for? Write down these intentions, and every time you are tempted to lean into safety, take out your intentions and ask yourself if you still believe them. If so, stay the course and don't give in. If not, rewrite them. Whatever you do, turn a deaf ear to the voice of fear and to the voice of comfort. Our proverbial release from prison will most certainly come only after some long hard years of feeling isolated and out of place. There is hope on the horizon, and you too will find a day when you will look at the people around you, some who have been there for years and others who just showed up, and confidently declare with light and joy in your eyes, "We did it!"

19

Acceptance

Happiness can exist only in acceptance.

—George Orwell

When my oldest child, macia, was in fifth grade, she called me into her room. She was sitting on her bed holding her knees in her arms, and she said there was something she needed to tell me. This extremely confident child was shaking and obviously nervous, so I reassured her that she could tell me anything and that nothing she could possibly say to me would make me love her any less. That comment seemed to be the courage she needed to tell me that she felt like she might be gay. I was wildly surprised by this declaration. I never saw it coming, but thankfully my work in difficult situations with people telling me very shocking things on a regular basis helped me keep my face and body calm and collected.

I don't remember my exact words, but I let her know that if she was indeed gay, it would not in any way change my feelings for her or my love for her. Sure, being a pastor of B-Side, a missional church supported largely by evangelicals, was going to be a little sticky, but from a standpoint of love and acceptance, I could not have cared any less. She will always be my girl, and I'll always be humbled and honored to have her in any form she is in. Love for a child should come with no asterisk.

After talking for a while, I asked why she was nervous to tell me this news since we have always had a great connection and I believe myself to be a pretty accepting and loving human being. Her response, which I remember verbatim, was, "I was afraid that you would hate me, and I was afraid that God would hate me." This child of mine grew up in the evangelical church, and the message she managed to receive and hear, which I can assure you never came from my lips, was that to be gay means rejection and the withholding of love. Not only that, but it meant that she was to be hated. It was in that moment I knew that for the rest of her childhood, and maybe even beyond, I was going to need to protect her from the very people I considered my tribe, my family, and my people.

For some reason I'd believed that because people had always seemed genuinely loving and kind to my daughter, that this new reality would not change anything—because after all, they knew her. She was a part of them. They were her people and she was their people. After she officially "came out" as a freshman in high school, it turns out . . . not so much.

First and foremost, I have to be honest and say we had to work through a lot as a family, which was extremely difficult. She was only ten when we'd had that first conversation. Her body was still developing; her hormones were all over the place. Doesn't every middle school girl believe she is gay at some point? Let's just say true acceptance turned out to be quite a process, because in our minds, as her parents, we wanted to carefully help her through puberty in order to see how true and real these feelings were. A word from experience: start with belief and work from there. Starting with skepticism creates problems. Lots and lots of problems that take years to recover from. An older, wiser me would now say, "If she is gay, accept, love, and protect. If it's just a phase, accept, love, and protect." For those of you who have never parented an LGBTQIA+ child, please know that it is impossible to understand the emotional challenges unless you live this reality. Understanding from a distance is different from understanding close up. It's one thing to be accepting in regular life and to show up to pride parades. It's a whole different ball of wax when it's your kid. Those reading this with kids who are not straight know exactly what I mean. That's not to come down on my lovely affirming friends; it's just true. There is a different level of emotion that you are forced to deal with. *Is this real? How can I keep them safe? What is our family going to think?* And so many other questions. All that to say, obstacle number one was within the walls of our own house.

Next—and this one was the most surprising—it was her youth group friends. Within just a matter of months they began distancing themselves from her, letting her know she was a sinner and in more than one situation sharing with her that her gayness was going to land her a permanent stay in the fiery pit of hell. Thank you for that, you little Christian teenage zealots. Not a single youth group friend stood up for her. Not a single youth group friend said, "I love you—period." They did like Christians tend to do when faced with uncomfortable situations. They pointed fingers, condemned, and disappeared. And here I thought we were so far past the bigotry that I saw when I was young.

As much as I was and honestly still am pissed at those youth group kids (and don't even get me started on the various youth leaders' choice to avoid the conversation at all costs and to not intervene in the slightest), and as much as I hated the actions of these young people, at least they were honest and forthcoming, which is more than I can say for most of the adult Christians in her life. Let me start by acknowledging that some of our closest friends who have been with us through thick and thin never once wavered in their love for my Macia. My forthcoming comments exclude them since they have shown over and over what true love and acceptance look like.

But most of the general Christian population avoids conflict by pretending they don't believe what they actually do believe. This bullshit idea that you can love without acceptance is total insanity. This idea that all the churchgoing adults in her life would share the sentiment that "We accept you" but then still call the way she was put on this earth a sin is manipulative, hurtful, and honestly horrific. The repeating words from pastors that she is welcome but she can't serve, be a pastor, or get married here actually mean that she is not at all welcome. This is the opposite of being welcome. It would be better if you just didn't let her in the building at all so she knew where she stood instead of using the old bait and switch of "Come on in, fill a seat, and feel free to toss a couple bucks in the offering plate. Fall in love with the people, be moved by the music, and oh, by the way, who you are puts you on the bottom of the hierarchy, so no to membership, no to leadership, and no to being yourself." They consistently chose the road of tolerance instead of acceptance. Being tolerated is much different than being accepted. I have no interest in your toleration of me, but I would love your acceptance. I am not convinced that love and tolerance go together.

Forgive me for getting a little punchy about this, but friends, this is my kid. Her name means "wished for," and Suzie and I have loved her since the idea of her came into our hearts. My kid is amazing. My girl is a powerhouse. My child is a difference maker. So yes, I am going to get a little worked up about this! But here is the amazing part of the story. Macia has stood up to every comment, every lost friendship, every judgmental and hateful post with such strength, such integrity, and such grace. Does she get pissy about it sometimes? Well, the apple doesn't fall far from the tree. But this young woman is some sort of spectacular. She had patience for me, her mother, our family and friends. She found new friends who love her—period. And she no longer considers the concept that the divine could hate her in any way, shape, or form.

I recently heard a podcast guest share that the phrase "coming out" gives the power to everyone else. It's like saying, "I am coming out to enter into your world." A better thought is that others are being invited in. It's saying, "This is who I am, and you are welcome to join with my true authentic reality. If you choose to do so, you will be blessed." Let's change National Coming Out Day to National Welcoming In Day. I pray for a day when people who are not straight no longer feel as if they have to come out of the closet but instead feel as if they are letting others into a vast and beautiful open space that is gorgeous and free.

I grew up in a household that was open and accepting in many ways but very closed-minded in others. One of my uncles showed up to every family function with his "friend," who just happened to also be a man. Everyone knew they lived together, but no one ever gave them the freedom to be themselves. Everyone knew it but pretended as if they didn't. Recently my mom texted me, letting me know that they were heading to the courthouse to be witnesses at the wedding. I put down my phone, sat down, and let a tear freely run down my cheek. I'm in my mid-forties, and for my entire life it was always my uncle and his "friend." I can't even fathom the pain of not being able to openly express feelings for a lover for over forty years. For the first time in my life, I will be able to meet my uncle and his husband.

Even during the height of my conservative church days, I never bought into the thought that being something other than straight was a sin. There were, however, many times when I chose to be silent in the midst of conversations, and for every one of those situations, I trust in God's forgiveness because that action, or lack thereof, I am confident is indeed a sin. Even though I have always been accepting, when being gay took on a name, everything changed. When being gay was my dear sweet beautiful daughter, no longer would I ever remain silent. And no longer will I ever accept a faith that is anything other than inclusive and affirming of everyone.

Bring It Home

As we work to find our faith again, it is extremely important to make decisions about what we truly believe. There is no pressure to get this "right" because our faith is ever evolving and may look different every single day. But when it comes to how we think about groups of people—the LGBTQIA+ community, people who have a different racial identity than we do, people who think differently about God than we do—it is vital that we not just decide what we believe in theory, but that we experience our beliefs in practice.

A God worth following is a God who accepts us—period. Not a God who accepts us *in spite of*, or a God who accepts us *even though*. If we can manage to believe in a God who accepts us unreservedly, we may just be able to live a life that is truly accepting toward others—not just in theory, but in practice.

20

Solitude

I never found the companion that was so companionable
as solitude.

—Henry David Thoreau

IN GENERAL, I WAS A pretty good kid who rarely got into trouble. I
suppose the truth is that I was an average kid who rarely got caught.
In the moments when I was frustrated with my parents, my brother,
or just life in general, I would sneak out the back patio door and
walk up the steep incline behind our house. It wasn't an easy climb,
but the payoff was well worth it. There was a rock up there that I
loved to sit on. When I looked out from it, I could see for what felt
like forever. It was a space that provided seclusion and solitude.
When I went there, no one knew where I was, and as I looked out,
everything seemed as if it was going to be okay. I never felt a great
need to talk through things; I just needed some time and space to
get some perspective. I used to practice the drums for hours each
day growing up, partially because I had a hunger to succeed and
partially because it was just me and the music. No one else for as
long as I wanted. In hindsight it is kind of humorous that my peace
came with so much noise.

As I grew older, this solitude I loved so much became more and more elusive as a spouse, a career, and children ultimately took most hours of my life. Whenever I commit to something, I commit to it all the way, and in my mind that meant giving my family and my career as much time as I possibly could. I rarely took any time to be by myself. And babies in the house took the option of practicing the drums for hours off the table. Early in our marriage Suzie would ask me every year what I wanted for my birthday, and I would always respond by saying, "I just want about an hour to go on a walk by myself." It was not so much to get away from everyone and everything as it was a desire to find the solitude and perspective that used to be so readily available. This was perplexing to my wife, who is an unapologetic extrovert, and it caused all sorts of difficult conversations and situations in our relationship over the years. I am happy to say, though, the older we get, the more we understand each other—to the point that solitude is now not only accepted but also encouraged!

Growing up Catholic meant peace and solitude were par for the course. After all, we had people like Saint Francis, Saint Patrick, and Saint Brigid, as well as many faith heroes who chose solitude as their superpower. If you have never been to a Catholic mass, the first thing you experience is silence. Every Sunday, as we walked into the church, it was quiet. No music, no talking, just silence. You could hear every footstep and every creak in the pews as congregants filed in. The priority was not on celebration, but on reverence and remembrance. As a boy I would sit in the pew, alone with about a hundred others, looking up at Jesus on the cross and scanning the walls to see the stations of the cross. I would get lost in thought about each one. The man carrying the cross for Jesus, the woman wiping his face, the crown of thorns. It is certainly fair to say that the beginning of my faith came from contemplation during those quiet spaces before mass began. Eventually the organ would start and the procession would begin, but only after the time of silence and reverence.

My first experience at a non-Catholic church was as opposite as is humanly possible. I was greeted with hearty handshakes and pleasantries. As I entered the lobby, it was filled with voices and laughter, and as I took my seat, worship music blared through the speakers. Everything was bright and loud—and the service hadn't even begun. Five minutes before the start of the service, a countdown began on the screen with some sort of weird tame techno music building anticipation before the live band showed up onstage, hitting the downbeat with intention and aggression. The leader would shout good morning and yell some words of encouragement not unlike the speeches I remember from my coach before a big basketball game in high school. The rule of the day was to play music loud enough that the congregation can't hear themselves sing. Moving images crossed the screen with words helping us to sing along. People clapped during and after each song before sitting down twenty minutes later to listen to announcements given by a bubbly and vibrant college student who prayed with intensity not unlike a karate master prepping to break a board in half.

We were then given the opportunity to give money to keep this show rocking into the future! The band played a tune that started calmly before a five-minute climb into super-intense repetitive singing. Eventually the music stopped and a man with khakis and a button-up shirt moseyed to center stage to make us laugh, cry, and ponder, with a full slideshow to exaggerate his points. After forty minutes he began a crescendo that culminated in another intense song before we were finally dismissed for more talking, greetings, and pleasantries. By the time it was over, I was exhilarated and worn the hell out!

The excitement obviously outweighed the negatives; I dove headlong into this type of church for the next couple of decades, working with teams of people to discover ways to better tap into all of our emotions and desires. Suzie and I even started our own Christian rock band that we toured the country with for over two years. Eventually, though, it all wore out, and I found myself sitting in the front row listening to another version of the five sermons I had heard a million times, desperately longing for that quiet Catholic church with Jesus on the cross, the stations on the walls, and all the peace, serenity, and contemplation.

After finally leaving the evangelical church, my first temptation was to become Catholic again. Unfortunately, my attempt at a return ended up being a polka mass, and although I appreciate my Polish heritage and constantly brag that my grandfather played in a professional polka band, that music fits much better in a bar, basement, or anniversary party than it does a church. I have stopped looking for that peace in churches and have since returned to the forest, the rivers, and the country roads.

The modern church uses a phrase that has haunted me for years. "We are created for community." Because I desired so desperately to fit in, I prayed and attempted for years and years to have friends in the church and to be a part of small groups. I felt like absolute horseshit over and over because I really struggle with friendships and I rarely desire to hang out with any humans other than Suzie and my kids. Sure, I enjoy hanging out with others from time to time, and I like to make people laugh, so that can be fun, but this deep intimate ongoing shit that I was being encouraged to partake in was nothing short of daunting. I felt like the worst Christian because I could never identify with the thought of being created for community.

Years after leaving the church, I ran into a former priest by the name of Scott Jenkins who is deeply rooted in Celtic Spirituality. As I spoke with him and podcasted with him, I felt something within me begin to reawaken. I felt a deep connection in our conversations about nature and solitude. And for the first time in my life, I freely asked the question, "Am I created for community?" The conclusion I have come up with is, absolutely!

The problem is, I have been thinking of community all wrong. Sure, for some people, like Suzie, being created for community with other people is absolutely who they are. If that girl has too much alone time, she can get a bit chippy, if you know what I mean. I am not created for community like that. That type of community is nothing short of exhausting. I'm sure all the introverts reading this can relate to me when I talk about a switch that suddenly goes off at social gatherings. I can hang in there for a while, but eventually it's like the light switch turns off and it is time for Matt to go home. Because of this, for years I thought I was broken. I wasn't able to live up to the expectation I experienced in modern church life. But my new friend Scott taught me that community can mean so much more than just human beings. We are deeply connected to nature, and although it is true that we can be in community with other humans, we also can be in community with all of creation. The first community we see in the Bible is two humans and the wilderness around them. And they all worked together in harmony until they started to believe that they were not truly created to be one with each other.

So, yes, I am created for community. I am created to be in community with all of creation. When I hop on my bicycle and ride for hours along country roads, I am not by myself. I am with the wind. I am with the sun. I am with the birds flying overhead. When I walk in the woods, I am not alone. I am with the trees. I am with the deer. I am with the clouds above. When I am in my kayak on a river, I am not alone. I am with the water. I am with the fish below me. I am with the sun in my face. My friends, we are never alone.

Over and over again, people have desired to be close to me because they have assumed things about me that simply are not true. They assumed that because I am a dynamic speaker and presenter that I would be a dynamic friend or counselor. And this wasn't on them; it was on me, because I would reiterate the things that were taught to me—that we are made for community with people. I would try to become friends with many of them, but people can see through inauthenticity, and eventually the relationship would fade away or end in hurt or disappointment. The truth is that all of us are created for community, but how we live that out can be wildly different. Some of us are created for relationships and connections, while others are created for solitude and space. Jesus shows us both. He had some great friends and also took a lot of time for himself. He was created for community and for community with creation, which on some level is true for all of us. In Jesus we can glean from whatever we need based on how we came into this world. For me, I was created for community with my Suzie, my kids, extended family a few times a year, friends every so often, and nature as much as humanly possible.

Bring It Home

In the words of Saint Patrick, one of my Catholic brothers,

> *Christ with me, Christ before me, Christ behind me,*
> *Christ in me, Christ beneath me, Christ above me,*
> *Christ on my right, Christ on my left,*

Christ when I lie down, Christ when I sit down,
Christ in the heart of every man who thinks of me,
Christ in the mouth of every man who speaks of me,
Christ in the eye that sees me,
Christ in the ear that hears me.

That is community enough for all of us.

21

Loss

How lucky am I to have something that makes
saying goodbye so hard.
—Winnie the Pooh

ONE OF THE ONLY CERTAIN things about life is death. Most everyone
is fearful of losing a loved one or losing their own life. And anyone
who is an adult has had to experience it on some level. Sometimes it
is soul crushing and confusing, while other times it seems almost
poetic. I have been at funerals where it felt more like a party, and I
have been at funerals where the sadness is so thick you can physically feel it. I have been at funerals where there were just a handful
of people, and I have been at funerals where there was barely enough
room for all the people who wanted to attend. No matter the cir-
cumstance, death is something that causes us to pause and think
every time we encounter it.

One of my first close experiences with death was when I taught
high school music in a small town right after college. About halfway
through the school year, I arrived at the building to a very somber
mood and was informed by the administrators that one of the students at the school had died from suicide. I had worked hard to make
the band room a place where kids could come if they needed to talk

or if they just needed some space to think, and for weeks the room was flooded with students trying to make any sort of sense of what happened to their classmate, their friend, their neighbor. Emotion was thick and raw. There were tears, and there was deep sadness, and all I could say was, "I am here, and this space is available for you." As soon as things started returning to normal and the small town was beginning to catch its collective breath, it happened again. A second student in a single year dying from suicide after the town had gone for years prior without a similar scenario. It felt like the students' broken ribs were just starting to heal when someone kicked them again. More tears, more questions, another funeral, and another life slipping needlessly to the other side.

A few years later at a church where my wife and I worked, a young family lost their wife and mother to a battle with cancer. She couldn't have been much older than forty, and she left behind a husband and two teenage girls. I remember the deep sadness I felt, especially being a father of two girls myself, but I couldn't pretend to understand the grief the family was enduring. Because the funeral was in a church, everybody did that bullshit of trying to make sense of it or trying to place God's will on this brutal situation when in reality an all-loving God would seem incapable of ripping a mother and a wife away from her family. *Agape* love doesn't inflict a death sentence on a young woman before she gets to see her girls graduate or get married. Even as I write this, I can still picture the husband's sad eyes as he walked into the sanctuary. He had asked Suzie and I to play music for the service, so we had a front-row seat for the grief as we sat on the stage facing the family for the entire funeral, watching all the emotion and heartache continue to unfold. All I could think was, *Why the hell are we putting them through this? They just lost her after a long exhausting battle, and now they have to expose their deepest wounds publicly in front of a bunch of people they go to church with.*

Several years after that heartbreaking moment, we were on staff at another church when the pastor informed us of a situation with a mother who was pregnant with twins. We, as a church, were praying from them because the pregnancy was not going well. When the time for delivery arrived, one child survived while the other did not. The doctor shared that the child who died hung on just long enough for the birth of the other to be safe and viable. A strange, poetic, and heart-wrenching story. How does a parent begin to deal with the complex emotion of the extreme joy of new life and the crushing brutality of death happening at the very same moment? Again, we provided music for the funeral. Every song felt like it was simply a battle of trying to hold back tears. The tiny casket, the parents holding hands, the child who survived, and the pastor fumbling for anything meaningful to say. I appreciated the fact that the pastor refrained from trying to make any sense of it, and he never once tried to put a positive spin on the situation.

Death came to my door once again when I was a prison chaplain. I was working an evening shift when I received a call from an upper-level security guard letting me know that I needed to call an inmate to my office to inform him that his mother had passed away. This man had been in prison for over twenty years and had to hear from a stranger that his mom had died. I asked him to sit down, looked him in the eyes, and shared with him news that I obviously knew would crush him. It did, and the proud, strong, imposing figure of a man crumbled in front of me, burying his head in his hands and weeping uncontrollably. I wasn't allowed to leave him there by himself, so I just sat silently with my hand on his shaking shoulder and waited until he was ready to make a phone call to his family.

Because the prison system is a mess, he couldn't even go to the funeral or view it virtually. The only thing afforded him was that his family could send in a video of the service and I could set up a private viewing time for him. Yes, he was there for a reason. Time in prison is a consequence for whatever it was he did. But that doesn't change the fact that death stole this man's mother and he would never get the opportunity to grieve in the way a human being needs to. The sadness is hard enough on its own, but when it is joined by the guilt of not being present for the last twenty years, I would imagine that weight is next to unbearable. When I would see him after his mother's passing, he seemed empty, stoic, and void of emotion. Like he built some sort of wall around himself to avoid showing any true feelings in a place where that was not well received.

Death is always hard, and every situation is unique. Some go through grief with grace while others never find the pathway back to any sense of normalcy. Some allow it ruin them while others use it to propel them. Both scenarios are understandable.

We will use token phrases like, "They are in a better place," and while I certainly hope that is true, I have no clue where they are. We celebrate, saying that "Today they are with God in paradise." I trust that in some way that's true, although I believe that phrase is simply an attempt to find comfort in the midst of grief. We go through our rituals, placing bodies in the ground or returning them to ashes. "Dust to dust, ashes to ashes," is what my priest would say growing up.

Death is a part of life. And in our faith circles we have spent a lot of time trying to make sense of it. Eternal dwelling places, streets of gold, mansions, and clouds have been created in the minds of the faithful. Fates have been placed on the heads of the deceased based on what they claimed to believe or not believe.

Libraries full of books have been written about the subject. And far too much of our religion has been focused on it. Escaping death instead of embracing or grieving it has been the narrative for far too long.

As much as we might try, we will be incapable of understanding this part of life. But what I am certain about is that it affords us the opportunity simply to be present. Simply to make ourselves available. We have this grand opportunity to shut our mouths and just be there. Not as someone who can relate or as someone who understands, but simply as someone who cares. There is no need for the clever phrases; they are usually more hurtful than helpful. There is no need for the token Bible verses; they just come across as belittling. Be sad with. Be angry with. Be confused with. Be shattered with. That is what is helpful. Just being with.

A friend of mine recently lost her college-age son. He was young, vibrant, and full of life and love. Those who love much and care deeply find the hurts in life heavy weights to carry. This young man made the decision that he no longer desired to bear such a burden. In the midst of unimaginable sorrow, my friend and her husband, within the first year of this devastating loss, posted a picture of themselves wearing black T-shirts with white lettering that simply said, "Fuck Grief." That made more sense to me than anything I ever heard or read on the subject because that felt real and honest.

Bring It Home

As we work to rediscover our faith in this challenging world, it is important that we recognize and honor the death we encounter along the way. Not as an opportunity to try and understand but as an opportunity to choose not to.

Religion has a black stain throughout history. It is a stain left on those who have been shattered emotionally only to have their sorrow and confusion explained away by some faith professional who thinks they have eternity figured out.

The best way to combat this past is to be honest in our suffering and to be present for others during their suffering. We don't understand. We don't need to understand. Sometimes the grandest faith and the most helpful spiritual practice is presence without understanding.

22

How to Believe

I am always doing what I can't do, yet in order that
I may learn how to do it.
—Vincent van Gogh

FOR YEARS I MADE ENDS meet by teaching private drum lessons. At my high point (or should I say at rock bottom), I was teaching around thirty budding rock stars the fine art of making organized noise. During the first lesson I would always ask them what it was about the drums that made them interested, what kind of music they liked, and what their goals were. Just about every student had some version of the same story about seeing or hearing a rock drummer from a popular band. They loved the music, were inspired by the drummer, and wanted to see if they had what it takes.

After that question I sat down and played a variety of different beats and honestly just showed off a bit so they knew the guy who was going to teach them was not some sort of wannabe hack, and when I stopped and saw their eyes bugging out of their heads (which honestly does not take much for a fifth grader), I let them know that they too could play the same way if they put in the time. Desire and even natural talent will only get you so far. Hard work and dedication to learning the craft is what is required to get good at anything.

Their faces would fall a bit at this point, and then I would inform them that for our first lesson all we were going to do was learn how to hold the drumsticks. I was quite the killjoy. Lesson two was reviewing the stick holding, followed by playing on a pillow. This is to ensure proper technique from the beginning. By lesson three they were finally allowed to hit a drum for the first time, but just one single drum and only a few times. It wasn't until the second month of lessons that they were allowed to actually attempt anything on the entire drum set.

A person would naturally assume that all their longing would lead to a great desire to practice. A person would assume that when the floodgate was released, the practicing would begin, and the journey toward rock stardom would be well under way. But a person would be wrong. The truth is, those little buggers would rarely pick up a pair of sticks in between lessons, and I would end up repeating the same things lesson after lesson, week after week, giving me a deep desire—in true rock star form—to kick over the drum set. It was like the movie *Groundhog Day* where every day was the same over and over again.

All this to say, my time as a drum instructor—for the sake of my soul and for the wellbeing of the students—was short lived. I learned during this time of my life that people are often unwilling to do that hard work necessary to accomplish their goals and dreams. Overnight success takes years and years of practice and preparation. My students could want to be rock stars all day long, but when it came down to it, most were unwilling to do the work it takes to accomplish the goals they set.

This laziness has the potential to creep into every area of life, including religion. Many people of faith choose to rely on the expert knowledge of pastors, priests, and leaders to be the source for their spiritual wellbeing. They don't have to worry about learning all that Bible stuff because the professionals have that locked down. Basically, all you have to do is show up week after week for the same thing over and over, just like my drum students. I can remember leaving church once as a young boy and asking my parents why we never read the dusty Bible in the closet. My mom responded that we don't have to because that's the priest's job. I didn't question her answer, and I certainly did not bother dusting off the Bible.

I personally stepped away from the Catholic Church because I wanted something that felt more alive and less routine, and I loved the fact that we were encouraged to read the Bible and explore things for ourselves. Eventually, though, I had a revelation that the Protestants were not all that different from the Catholics. Sure, the music was louder and there were no robes, but at the end of the day the whole concept was pretty similar. Yes, we were allowed and even expected to read the Bible for ourselves, but only if we were going to understand it in the correct way. And even though we didn't call the guy up front "Father," we still expected him to have all the answers. All we had to do was get the basics down about God, Jesus, heaven, hell, and salvation and show up to church each Sunday. The rest could be left up to the professionals. The emergence of the megachurch has made this reality even more obvious; we can slip in and out of church without being noticed and without any expectations whatsoever. Let the professionals do their thing as we give our obligatory hour to God each week. The people feel great, the professionals get paid . . . what could possibly be wrong with that?

Unlike the Catholic Church, these Protestant professionals have not been able to agree on much of anything. Sure, the Catholics have an unhealthy hierarchy that forces conformity, but the lack of this structure hasn't historically provided better results. There are thousands of Protestant denominations that have all come about by living up to their name. The word *protestant* comes from the original protest against the Catholic Church by Martin Luther. They have continued their protests for hundreds of years and now are quite the fractured group. What was originally supposed to be a group of people bringing love, hope, and freedom to the world has turned into factions arguing about who has the correct interpretation of an ancient collection of writings. For years one of the biggest knocks against Protestant Christianity has been and continues to be that they can't get along.

Unfortunately, not only did the differing opinions lead to new denominations, they also led to some horrific acts of violence and injustice. John Calvin had a man beheaded because he was a "heretic." Lutherans would drown Anabaptists because of their differing opinions on baptism. And the violence between Protestants and Catholics throughout the years has been nothing short of appalling. All of this because a few men at the top believed they had the corner on the truth. And although I do not like to generalize, too often when men are afforded too much power, they respond with violence against those who oppose them.

We have all heard the phrase "blind faith" when talking about religion. There is certainly a good deal of truth in the concept. We will never be able to see God, so in order to believe in the divine, our faith will in many ways indeed be blind. But blind faith in humans is unnecessary because we can see them. I don't need to blindly follow a pastor or a political leader or anyone else. I can put in the time and effort to discover what they believe and stand for and make a logical decision about being connected to them or the organization they lead. Blind faith in people has gotten us into a lot of trouble, especially in religious circles. And I don't think that is what Jesus was

asking of us. Jesus rarely asked anyone to believe in him but instead
asked people to follow him. By following Jesus, they got to know and
understand who he was and what he stood for. And consistently,
without fail, he stood up for the underdog, stood against oppression,
and stood for love, peace, and freedom. I can fool anyone for an hour
with a microphone in front of my face, but I can't fool anyone who
lives with me for years. Suzie, my kids, and close friends are the ones
who truly know who I am, what I stand for, and what I struggle with.

All great movements of change start from the ground up, and
this movement away from harmful Christianity is being led by the
people in the pews who refuse to blindly follow people leading organizations that, unlike Jesus, are exclusive and not welcoming to
everyone. People are beginning to do the work of making discoveries
for themselves about what they are a part of. Many are deciding not
to stay, while others are deciding to bring up important and challenging conversations. Some leaders and communities are open to
these conversations, others are dismissive, but at the end of the day it
will be the well-thought-out voices and actions of the people that
win out. History proves this over and over.

I have no doubt that there is change on the horizon, which I am
excited to watch unfold. But I am concerned that we will simply continue to repeat history in new ways if we are not careful. I am worried that this movement of faith will start from the bottom, as it
already has, before being passed off to the "experts." Once again. The
movement Jesus started was passed not from his hand to the hands
of the experts, but from his hands to the hands of the ordinary people who followed him. Not to start some sort of well-organized, powerful organization, but to start a bottom-up love revolution.

The greatest lessons I have been learning in my post-evangelical
life have not been how to defend my new concepts of belief or how

to reinterpret the Bible through a new lens. All that leads to is more of the same shit we have seen for so many years. The lessons I have been working on are things like becoming a better listener, learning to meditate, being present in every moment, and discovering how to be true to myself. It's as if I am picking up the drumsticks again for the first time, remembering the basic foundations before jumping into an Afro-Cuban samba to land an audition. But remembering the foundation is just the first step. If we don't take the time to follow Jesus and we just pass the responsibilities off to others, we may never see that vast power our faith can have in the world around us. Power to flip things upside down, power to overcome injustice, power to see love win over and over again, and power to allow others to be seen, heard, and cared for.

Bring It Home

My youngest child has some wonderfully unique beliefs. We have some of the most fascinating conversations. Sometimes when they say things, I think, *That sounds crazy,* and then I remember that my faith is built on the concept of a person literally rising from the dead.

This kiddo is intentional about faith, fascinated by faith, engaged in faith, and couldn't care less if it makes any sense to their father. This is their story and their experience. After listening to dad talk in front of people about Jesus for years and years, they have decided that Christianity is not a valid path for them. We have, however, agreed on a few points of commonality in our journeys. First, faith has to be uniquely our own. Second, faith should make the world around us better. And third, our faith should be inclusive.

As you journey back home, attempting to make sense of your spirituality, be intentional about the right things, not the right answers. The right things are the foundations of love and hope, which can be expressed in a variety of ways. No one would ever argue that Mother Teresa was any better or worse than Mahatma Gandhi. Their religious beliefs were quite different, but their foundations were exactly the same. In the end, I think it's much less about what we believe and much more about how we believe.

23

Discovery

We keep moving forward—opening new doors,
and doing new things—because we're curious.
And curiosity keeps leading us down new paths.
—Walt Disney

I WAS SITTING AT A coffee shop with a local pastor who reached out to me wanting to hear about my views on the LGBTQIA+ community. This is something that has happened more than a few times over the past couple of years simply because people want to understand how I can still consider myself a Christian and affirm the LGBTQIA+ community when, in their words, "the Bible is clear on the issue." To be honest, there has not been a single conversation like this in which a pastor has tried to change my mind or set me straight. They have all been great conversations in which the goal seems to be understanding, not judgment. And in all the conversations I have had, the pastors have identified that they too were thinking through and wrestling with it. In this particular conversation, the pastor said to me at one point, "But if I change my mind on this, what is next? It is a slippery slope." To which I responded, "It certainly is."

The word that has been widely accepted to define a Christian person's rethinking of faith is *deconstruction*. Although I am not a huge fan of labels, I do understand the need, and this word does seem to describe quite well what I personally have gone through. I bought into a carefully curated set of beliefs that has been developed over thousands of years. The moment I began to question this well-constructed theology was the moment deconstruction began. My experience began with questioning conservative Christian views on homosexuality. From there it went to questioning beliefs on heaven, hell, and atonement. After that it was the infallibility of the Bible—that it has to be perfect in order to be valuable. At that point I slid all the way down the slide until I had very little left of my faith, causing me to question the existence of God altogether.

This has been a brutal process that has caused a great amount of grief, loss, and lament. I remember sitting by myself at one point, feeling angry and alone wondering if I had bought into a lie that defined my life for the past forty years. And not just any lie, but a lie that I willingly and strongly perpetuated. A lie that I shared on stages in front of tens of thousands of people. That was a very large pill to swallow, and it hurt all the way down. But eventually, after some borderline depression, a shattered career, and the loss of several close friends, I reached what felt like the bottom. The slope finally leveled off enough that I could find my footing, stand up, and look around to see where I was. And what I saw was something very exciting. In front of me was a canvas that was expansive and blank. A canvas on which I could draw or paint anything I wanted. And a canvas with which I was free to mess up and start over as many times as I need to. Faith was never meant to be a destination. Like a beautiful flowing river, it is meant to be ever moving and ever changing.

Another word that has attached itself to Christianity recently is the word *progressive*. Unfortunately this word, for many, has come to mean *liberal*. It also has a prideful overtone, as if those who are progressive are further along the path than those who are not. But the word *progressive* simply means to develop slowly step-by-step. For me personally that progression started in the Catholic Church before moving to the evangelical church. Not because God was absent from the Catholic Church, but simply because my life was changing, so my expression of faith also needed to change. I then progressed from there to a medium-security prison as a chaplain. Again not because God moved or changed, but because I did. Now I experience faith apart from any specific organization, not because any of them are necessarily bad or ungodly, but simply because I continue to develop step-by-step. At one point in my faith journey a couple of decades ago, I honestly believed that I had reached a peak where I had discovered the ultimate truth. The reality is that I was just lacing up my hiking boots and hadn't even started walking to the mountain.

Now that I have found my way to the bottom of my slippery slope of faith (at least for now), I have started looking around for other slippery slopes to slide down. Where else in my life is my perspective off, or lacking authenticity? It has been a wild ride of rethinking life, career, friendships, family, love, and humanity. I never again want to feel as if I have somehow arrived. It is much more fulfilling to live as a work in progress, always hoping and believing for something better.

On this road of discovery, one of the things I have realized is that people and organizations have viewed my talents and abilities as an opportunity to promote themselves and their mission. The troubling part about this is not their actions, but my willingness to go along with it. When they said, "We need you to be like us," over and over again I said a word that often gets me into trouble: "Sure."

I went from playing for incredible jazz groups to playing Christian rock music, which, as I write this, makes me cringe. I went from loving solitude to being constantly surrounded by people. I went from accepting to excluding. I gave up friendships with really amazing human beings for friendships with people who had agendas. When I sacrificed in these ways, the slope did indeed become slippery—and not in a good way. As I tried to be, act, and perform in the ways everyone else desired, every single decision I made became questionable, and every relationship I had suffered. I began to notice a pattern.

People would meet me for the first time and love me. They would want to do anything for me, would want to follow my lead, and would want to spend as much time as they could with me. Then after a number of months or years they would start to become very disappointed in me. I felt like I was letting down one person after another, and I was beginning to wonder what the hell was wrong with me. Like most of humanity, my first reaction was to blame them. But the reality is, I was showing them a caricature of myself. They would fall in love with that version of me but over time begin to see who I really was, which was contrary to what they loved about me. This happened with people, and it also happened with organizations and churches. As a youth speaker I was eventually chastised and uninvited, after being the top-rated speaker at a camp, when I revealed pieces of my true self. At the prison, they eventually put me on unpaid administrative leave before I willingly resigned because my actions eventually showed who I truly was, which was not the person fit for the job. I was dismissed from B-Side because I started to be true to myself, and that wasn't the version of me the leadership team I put in place liked.

As I find myself screaming down all these slopes, I am tempted to do what every little kid has done on the playground. I am tempted to grab the sides of the slide and stick my foot down to stop myself from sliding any further. But as I look over my shoulder, I am reminded of a place I no longer want to be, so I slowly pick up my feet and release my grasp to let my body slide down further.

Just as I was about to begin work on a big project for an anti-human-trafficking organization, I was invited to their staff retreat. At the beginning of the retreat I looked at everyone in the room and said, "I am good at what I am going to be doing for this organization. And because I am good at it, you, like others have in the past, might assume things about me that are not true. I need to let you know that under this confidence and ability is a guy who struggles with relationships. Underneath all the passion you will see in front of groups of people is an introvert who needs a lot of time by himself. Underneath the success you will see a lot of failures along the way. I am not here to make friends; I am here to join with all your incredible talents to make a difference in this world." They all thanked me for my honesty and simply moved on with the meeting. It turns out it isn't all that hard to be honest, and most times, people will have no problem with it.

After I chatted with the pastor about the LGBTQIA+ community, he kindly let me know that my family and I are always welcome at his church. I thanked him but told him that I didn't believe that was true since I have family members who are not straight. If it is not a safe space for them or a space where they have the same opportunities as everyone else, we actually are not welcome. He seemed to understand, we shook hands, and I headed up to the counter to buy a couple of donuts for my kids. The man behind the counter attended the pastor's church and overheard our conversation. He looked me in the eye and said, "I completely agree with everything you said." The slide is always more fun if you have some friends to go down it with!

Bring It Home

When you start to rethink parts of your faith and life—or, as in my case, all of it—there may be times when it feels like everything is slipping through your fingers. You may sense that your very foundation is crumbling underneath you. But a foundation that crumbles is one that wasn't built very well in the first place. Have you ever been up in a tall building like the Sears Tower in Chicago? Near the top you can actually feel the building sway with the wind. This is by design. If it were built too firmly a storm could destroy it; but with the ability to sway back and forth, although it may feel a little scary, it is actually much safer. That's not a bad metaphor for faith and life. If it is built too tight, without room for any flexibility, it will eventually crash to the ground. But with enough flexibility, it is allowed to adjust to whatever comes at it.

As challenging as rethinking and reimagining faith and life can be, rest assured that if you approach the process with humility and hope, the ride can be invigorating. So lean back, put up your feet, and enjoy!

Conclusion

FORTY YEARS AFTER THE RED station wagon first ushered me into my hometown, I decided to take a road trip with Suzie and my children to spend a little time in the place that acted as a foundation to who I have become. My parents moved away when I was in college, and I did not stay in touch with any of my childhood friends. We all went our separate ways and lost touch other than the occasional Facebook like. The four of us grabbed some coffee, hopped in the car, and set out for the journey I had taken many times. After exiting the freeway, we passed through the first small town of the journey, Sparta, nodding at the huge Spartan mascot in front of the school. We went through the town of Cataract, which was the place my dad would always call an eyesore as we drove through. On through Viroqua, which has become a haven for young hipster organic farmers but to me represents the team I played my final basketball game against. And then finally the lefthand turn across the bridge that takes us over the mighty Wisconsin River. Just beyond that bridge is the sign: BOSCOBEL. POPULATION 2,662.

The town has had a few upgrades, including a new gas station and some businesses that did not exist all those years ago. But for the most part it is the same, only older and a bit more run-down. The Dairy Queen and the Unique Cafe where I treated my family to lunch were starting to show significant signs of aging. The historic Boscobel Hotel, where the Gideon Bible began and where JFK once stayed, is still there, still closed other than the bar, and still appears abandoned. Most of the places I remember from my childhood remain, but they are older and less attractive than I recall.

As I headed out of town to the east on Old C toward my childhood home, I passed the super-maximum-security prison that was a story of great controversy shortly after my departure. The forest where I rode my dirt bike, shot bottle rockets at friends, and drank beer stolen from my buddy's nearby house is now home to the worst criminals in our state. My friends' childhood homes remain. Shawn's house, where I blew up the mailbox with a two-liter pop bomb; Matt's house, where I crashed my mom's moped going over a homemade jump. And Brandon's house, where Wiffle ball legends were made. All still there, just older and weary with age.

I turned up the hill that I was forced to walk down during the winters when the bus couldn't climb the icy slope. I drove past the home of the school bus bully, Hans, and the pretty older girl, Dawn, who had bangs standing a half-foot above her forehead because I grew up in the eighties. As I came over the crest of the hill that marked relief back when we had to ride our bikes up it, I could see the mailbox just before the old sledding trail. I'll never forget taking Suzie down that hill when we first started dating. As she screamed at the bottom of one of the most death-defying sledding experiences I'd had up to that point, she stood up, left her sled in the snow, and stomped up to the house without saying a word. I don't think she enjoyed it as much as I did.

As I pulled up beside my childhood house, it didn't look as I remembered it. The palace that I grew up in, where so many memories were made, now just looked like someone else's old house. Still there, but not really. As we exited the town after our short visit, I had a bittersweet feeling in my gut. There was a piece of me that missed that little town, and for maybe the first time I felt an understanding of why many of my classmates chose it as the place to stay, raise families, and grow older. But mostly I felt happy that I left years ago so the places that hold my childhood could remain majestic in my mind.

As we bring it home to learn the valuable lessons life has taught us, it's important to remember that it is the memories and the stories that are important, not the places where they happened. A building is temporary, but experiences are eternal and can never be taken away, only passed along and given new life.

We give a lot of value to the stories of Jesus and his followers that we read about in the Bible. But are they any more important than our own stories? Is it more impactful to glean from someone else's story or to learn from our own? I can only speak for myself and say that stories experienced are always more meaningful than stories heard or read. I am not advocating that we dismiss the Bible, only that we use the story it holds alongside the story we are currently living.

I dream of a day when we stop living other people's stories and start experiencing our own. I pray for a day when we stop living in the past and start embracing the present. Very few of us feel that our stories hold much value because we are constantly comparing ourselves to others whom we believe to be more profound or more important. At the end of the day, our stories are what we have, and unless we take time to enjoy and value the journey we are on, we really won't have much to offer the world around us. Your story is the one that matters the most to you. And how it interacts with the stories of people around you is where the real magic happens.

I trust that if we all stop looking outside our own lives to find ourselves, our lived experiences will create a more authentic and beautiful world to exist in. Be bold enough to live your life with passion, and be brave enough to trust your journey of faith. Maybe the key to life and faith is found in the place it has always been.

Maybe we can find God by finding ourselves.

Acknowledgments

It would be impossible to thank everyone who had something to do with this book since the idea came to my mind over a decade ago, but I will certainly do my best.

Special thanks first and foremost to my strong, beautiful, patient, and grace- filled wife Suzanne who experienced every start, stop, and re-start of this project and who listened to all of my excitement and frustrations during the process.

To my kids Macie and Auggie who never complained openly when dad was taking up evenings to write.

I have had some wonderful friends along this journey, specifically Kat and Ryan Sherman, John and Melissa Kleven, and Kelly Spencer, who were guinea pigs for all of my stories around camp fires, in congregations, and at concerts. Your laughter, response, or lack thereof was a great help in knowing which stories to include.

Mom and Dad, what an incredible journey we have had together. You continue to inspire me every day.

David Morris, my publisher and newfound friend at Lake Drive Books, "thank you" could never be enough for the opportunity you have given me.

To everyone who listened, encouraged, made suggestions, or showed up in the pages of this book, this project is not just mine; there is a piece of all of us in it.

And finally, to Boscobel: you will always have a piece of my heart.

About the Author

Matt Kendziera is a full-time speaker, podcaster, writer, and creator. He is the host of the *Chasing Goodness* podcast, engaging authors, activists, and influencers on questions that most people run from. He's also a collaborator with several other incredible organizations such as Fierce Freedom, Rachel's Challenge, Ashoka, Soularize, Celtic Way, and others. Matt currently lives in rural Wisconsin with the love of his life, Suzie, and his two teenage children. Learn more and follow Matt at mattkendziera.com.